Santiago Calatrava

Alexander Tzonis

Santiago Calatrava
The Poetics of Movement

Principal photography by
Paolo Rosselli

UNIVERSE

First published in the United States of
America in 1999
by UNIVERSE PUBLISHING
A Division of Rizzoli International
Publications, Inc.
300 Park Avenue South
New York, New York 10010

99 00 01 02 / 10 9 8 7 6 5 4 3 2 1

Design by
Joseph Cho and Stefanie Lew
Binocular, New York

Printed in Italy

Library of Congress
Cataloging-in-Publication Data

Tzonis, Alexander.
Santiago Calatrava: the poetics of movement
/ Alexander Tzonis.
          p.   cm.
Includes bibliographical references.
ISBN 0-7893-0360-4
1. Calatrava, Santiago—Criticism and
interpretation. 2. Architecture, Modern—
20th century. 3. Civil engineering—Spain—
History—20th century. I. Calatrava,
Santiago. II. Title.
NA1313.C35T9723 1999
720'.92—dc21   99-34196 CIP

All photographs copyright © Paolo Rosselli,
except the following:
Copyright © Heinrich Helfenstein: pages 10,
50 (sketch), 98, 117 (sketches), 172 (sketch),
204 (all), 223, 226;
Copyright © Sergio Belinchon: pages 167, 171,
172 (right), 173 (left and right)

Contents

Acknowledgments

I am grateful to Dr. Joseph Press, consultant to the book.

I also wish to acknowledge my debt to my critic and partner, Dr. Liane Lefaivre.

Santiago and Tina Calatrava were most generous in offering their collaboration. I am thankful for their care and inspiration. Special thanks to Paolo Rosselli, whose art was most inspiring while I worked on this book, and to Thomas Neurath, Kim Marangoni, Anthony Tischauser, and Sandrine Do Couto. I profited more than I can say from the invitation to spend a semester at MIT lecturing on design creativity, and I am grateful to Stan Anderson for his hospitality and for generating the best conditions for my research. This book also profited from the opportunity I had to lecture on the occasion of Calatrava's exhibition at the Israel Museum of Science in Haifa, and I owe much to Professor Zvi Dori and Dr. Rifca Hashimshony for their invitation and the long discussions with them about architecture and technology. Special thanks to Professor F.H. Schroeder, Micha and Talma Levin, to all members of the Design Knowledge Systems Research Center of TUD and, in particular, Asaf Friedman and Marijke Troost, to my secretary Janneke Arkestijn, for giving cheerful help and structure in countless matters. I owe thanks to Elizabeth Johnson, my editor at Universe, for bridging the Atlantic with insightful advice and effective support.

Throughout the years, Robert Berwick's friendship was a great encouragement and enlightenment; this book is dedicated to him, with love.

Introduction
Chrysalis

In a century dominated by specialization and fragmentation, Santiago Calatrava is one of the few designers who can be called universal. His numerous buildings, engineering projects, sculptures, and furniture designs consistently create a unique poetics of morphology that merges structure and movement. He transgresses the artificial distinctions between art, science, and technology, between reflection and action, between memory and creation, between problem-solving and wonder, in order both to posit a cultural vision permeating personal and professional lives, and to establish a new paradigm for practice.

Within this new paradigm, Calatrava selectively recalls established knowledge, then reuses and reinterprets it to serve each project's requirements. He casts seemingly hackneyed analogies in a new light. He critically reassesses architectural rules and deepens our understanding of more fundamental, more comprehensive problems of architecture. He invites us to rethink form, construction, and use of buildings by breaching current professorial routines and by overcoming existing barriers between professional institutions. His sculpture serves as a research laboratory for highly technical projects. His technical infrastructure projects, in turn, offer the text and plot for highly abstract aesthetic essays, sculpture, and engineering techniques that promote cultural quality, life, and meaning in the human community.

Calatrava's designs work on three levels. First, they solve problems by providing optimal schemes. These solutions, in turn, represent the core beliefs and desires that explain the designs. And finally, Calatrava's design solutions

encourage us to question where these beliefs and desires come from and why they are essential to humanity. Calatrava responds to all three issues. His basic design strategy is to make the search for optimal solutions, the discipline of critical inquiry, and the spirit of experimentation and adventure work together in the same scheme. His projects are unique because they satisfy views not through compromise but through a higher level of synthesis. This requires not only an excellent grasp of multiple domains but also the cognitive competence to create. The offspring of this process is a new type of design artifact: an amalgam of sculpture and tool, a new, broader definition of technology, and a new type of contemporary practice for architects, engineers, and artists. By overcoming the borders separating art, architecture, and engineering, Calatrava broadens our collective understanding of the artificial environment and provides new ways to improve cities and landscapes and the human communities within them.

To present Calatrava's unique practice, this book starts with the immediate surroundings of his youth—including the post–May 1968 crisis of European architecture and the technological culture of the Swiss Federal Institute of Technology in Zurich. We will see how Calatrava's germinal iconoclastic experiments with structure and movement sprang out of a long historical tradition. Since antiquity, most architects, engineers, and artists have sought to make structures stable and enclosures secure. Some, however, have also sought to make them break loose, grow, and fly. To paraphrase Henri Bergson, they have tried to "awaken the chrysalis" in them. Rather than submitting to constricting dogmas, Calatrava restores design as a drive for life.

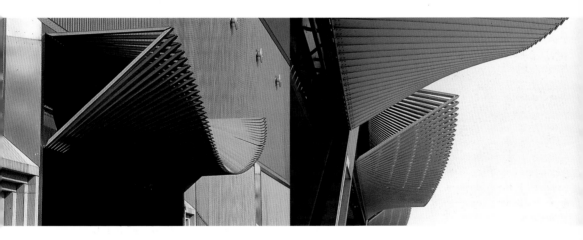

Above
Detail views of the folding door
mechanism for the Ernsting
Warehouse (4)

Facing page
Shadow Machine (14) in motion

Calatrava's projects recall the way the body of a complex living organism is put together. This is one of the reasons his bridges, observation towers, and building complexes fit and enhance the landscape like enormous organisms growing out of it or living within it. His forms, however, are not mimetic. His is not an "organic style." His schemes, rather, draw on nature, taking cues from the way the skeleton, the circulatory system, and the skin of organisms—especially the human body—function and flourish. In searching to develop a morphology of movement, he also draws dramatic significance from the body's acrobatic action—the dancer's gravity-defying gestures— to capture the shape of change and immerse it in a world in flux. As a result, Calatrava's structures, when embedded in the landscape like a tree, tend to enhance that land-scape's own uniqueness rather than subjugate its character. When placed in forgotten, peripheral parts of a city, Calatrava's creations bring about hope and renew desire.

As with any structure, Calatrava's projects operate on three levels simultaneously: as constructions, or how stable they are and how well they resist disintegration; as containers (also referred to as vessels or conduits), or how successfully they accommodate people and their activities; and as envelopes, or how adequately they cover a place. Calatrava has contributed significantly to all three aspects of structure. Unquestionably, the quality of his designs re-sults from collective thinking and collaborative effort. His success is due to the integration of his many skills and tal-ents, all of which contributed to the projects. Calatrava is uniquely able to encompass many kinds of knowledge, to think on a universal level, and to be endlessly inventive.

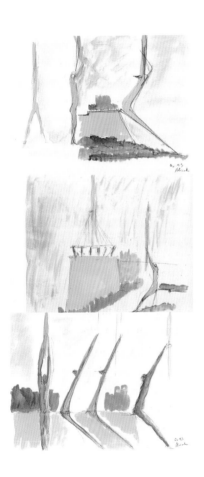

Above and facing page
Sketch studies for the Alicante
Tower (35)

Calatrava's explosive creative career has few parallels in the history of architecture. It is a labyrinth of schemes and solutions that expand, mutate, and merge in a whirlpool of multiplying design ideas that defy periodization and confound the historian and the critic. This study begins with his early projects, the first trials with optimal designs using materials and geometry. During the years that follow, these nascent ideas are expanded and recombined to fit more complex programmatic requirements and more challenging environments. Design strategies develop that call for ever more efficient and effective components—strategies that satisfy complex themes of design and movement while always embracing, even celebrating, the most difficult sites. Increasingly, as the complexity of the projects grows and the sophistication of their technology advances, the work manifests a tendency to produce the wildest metaphors. As Liane Lefaivre observes, borrowing a concept from Freud, Calatrava invites us, in much the same way filmmaker Luis Buñuel did, to experience "dream-work," or structures breaking free from the static world through a different kind of movement—one that generates possible worlds and fulfills a wish, a desire.[1]

Beyond problem-solving, critical inquiry, the spirit of adventure, and "dream-working," Calatrava's work has another dimension. Behind the obsession with form, structure, and movement that characterized his earlier years is an enduring passion for philosophical inquiry. Reminiscent of Spinoza, Calatrava seems intent on defining a moral system for human action and desire by way of geometric reasoning.[2] Within all the lines, planes, and solids is a vision of a better life.

Chapter One
Schools without Walls

Calatrava's œuvre resists description by way of conventional terminology: "invention" ignores the traditions he emerges from, "mechanics" reduces the range of values he embraces, and "structure" is oblivious to the profound qualities of movement in his work. In an era of division of labor and intellectual individualism that advances single-minded points of view, Calatrava demonstrates how, without failing to exploit the efficiency and effectiveness of specialization and personal expression, one can counteract their destructive impact, which breaks apart the cohesion of community and the coherence of consciousness. Each of his projects is a dialogue between the divisive traditions of thought and the insular habits inherited from the conflicts and competitions of history.

The appearance of Galileo's new science of mechanics was crucial in shaping contemporary design thinking.[1] The new world model, which rebuked archaic cosmological dogmas by creating a novel technology for structures, gave primacy to optimal efficiency and threatened to marginalize the conventional architecture of the time. Also crucial to the development of contemporary design and to what has been called functionalist and modernist architecture was a new wave of criticism against the architectural conventions of the late seventeenth century. Historians have identified this critical movement as *rigorism*.[2] Rigorism sought a new belief system to legitimize the old institution of architecture without subjugating it completely to the new one—engineering. It proposed stripping down buildings to their barest elements, eschewing all ornamentation, and giving visual primacy to a building's structural and mechanical elements, with which engineers were exclusively concerned. In this manner, architecture—according to Carlo Lodoli, a Franciscan friar known to some as "the Socrates of architecture" for his learned and eloquent diatribes[3]—could achieve "eternal youth" and a status equal to engineering.

While the new science of mechanics saw design as a highly efficient problem-solving process that maximized benefits and minimized costs, rigorism perceived it as a way of explaining—in an implicit, nonverbal, and figurative way—how the structure of a building worked, based on the new beliefs and desires related to the Galilean model. Thus rigorism updated the explanatory-learning role of architecture, which since the dawn of civilization has attached meaning to the components of a building, linking them to higher epistemological and moral ideas. The emerging division between optimizing products through calculation and intimating explanations through image, which, up to the Renaissance, with few exceptions, did not require a deep division of labor, now split design into two separate, specialized professional institutions: engineering and architecture. Despite numerous objections to this new system, only a small minority of designers continued to resist it successfully in professional practice. This tiny minority gave way to a rare lineage of architects, including Antonio Gaudí, Pier Luigi Nervi, Felix Candela, and R. Buckminster Fuller. Calatrava, too, belongs to and has excelled within this extraordinary tradition of syncretists. The significance of Calatrava's contribution comes out of the fact that today the cost—cultural and intellectual, if not economic—of many of these accepted divisions far exceeds the benefits. The division is increasingly not only a

source of delusion and conflict, but also a hurdle to
innovation. Thus, the need to make the various branches
of practice work together in a community of design
appears to be an urgent one.

Calatrava demonstrates his syncretist talents in another
way, as well. Rigorism viewed solidity as the most significant factor contributing to a project's efficiency. The
Galilean model, however, was applicable to other aspects
of projects besides standing solidly, such as containing and
covering activities, people, and objects. The model, there-
fore, could spread from construction to what we might
call the vessel (or container) and envelope (or covering)
parts of a project, and it did. But within the spirit of division of labor and intellectual individualism, most designers extending this model have been focusing on a single
aspect, a single part only. Calatrava, faithful to his univer-
salism, integrates all three into a design synthesis by fusing
their respective roles. But he also adds to them a fourth:
movement.

Calatrava introduces movement into the three aspects of
buildings we mentioned before: construction, vessel, and
envelope. Through them, movement plays a functional or
symbolic role. The project's parts move or serve moving
objects, or they convey the idea of movement figuratively.
This reframing of basic structural elements in terms of
movement places Calatrava alongside a historically significant group of architects, engineers, and artists who, for
utilitarian, cognitive, or aesthetic reasons have tried to
incorporate time, process, and transformation in their
designs.

What is fascinating about Calatrava's engagement with these issues and his commitment to rethinking design is that they evolved during a time when the role of technology (as well as mechanics and rigorism in construction) as a problem-solving process had entered a deep crisis. Rigorism in particular, by reducing tradition to superstition, context to irrelevance, and curiosity to lack of focus, encouraged an oversimplifying, detached frame of mind whose formidable barriers would pervade the subsequent architectural practice. Rather than eternal youth, it brought about decay. By the time Calatrava was a young man, rigorism had been exhausted. It had reduced the intellectual role of architecture to the trifling task of exhibiting the obvious in construction. Rather than using structures and technology as a means for reflection, meditation, or exploration, as it did during the nineteenth and the first part of the twentieth centuries, by the end of the 1960s rigorism meant indulging in technophilic and exhibitionist postures and embracing the banality of structure.

In 1951—the year of Calatrava's birth—work was beginning on a building that would profoundly influence the future architect and his discipline. Shocking an architecture community whose goal at the time was primarily to fulfill postwar reconstruction needs within a rigorist framework, Le Corbusier's chapel at Ronchamp foreshadowed the crisis to come. The building, with its irregular, rough-hewn walls and massive slab roof, was seen as an anomaly. Upon its completion in 1955, the leading British historian and critic Nikolaus Pevsner announced that Ronchamp, as the building came to be known, heralded the arrival of a "new irrationalism." Its seemingly erratic

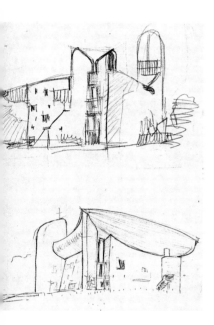

Above
Calatrava's sketches of Notre-Dame du Haut, Ronchamp, by Le Corbusier

and arbitrary configuration challenged contemporary routines and clichés of design. Its unruly form suggested that the arbitrary fixation on elementary Euclidean shapes and the exposition of construction, both derived from the rigorist dogma, were, by the middle of twentieth century, obsolete. They manifested only the obvious and the trivial. Ronchamp offered a puzzling and irregular, yet intelligent silhouette that reverberated through the site, echoing the surrounding landscape. It was the skin rather than the skeleton that achieved this effect and emphasized movement and adventure over stability and didacticism. Ronchamp was a challenge—a new approach to shaping space and to sharing structure and movement, a celebration rather than a subjugation of the landscape—and it would later play a critical role in the personal, artistic, and professional development of a then quite young Calatrava.

A descendant of aristocratic Spaniards and converted Jews, Santiago Calatrava grew up in Benimamet, a small village next to the diverse and culturally rich city of Valencia. The 1900 edition of the Baedeker travel guide describes the approach to Valencia by train as a landscape of blooming *huertas*, whitewashed cottages, wheat fields, and palms, the "shining dark-blue, white 'azulejo-domes' appearing 'in the distance.'" Upon crossing the Guadalaviarí River, visitors encounter castles that recall a former royal city. Valencia was founded by the Greeks and later occupied variously by the Romans, Arabs, Moors, and Goths, and, in the thirteenth century, hosted a large Jewish population. Eventually, it declined into an agrarian center. During the nineteenth and twentieth centuries, despite its royal past, Valencia played an important role in numerous republican uprisings. It was here that the last remnants of the Republican Party found refuge, and ultimately surrendered, after the fall of Catalonia to the Franco army in 1939. It was only in the 1950s, however, under the Franco regime, that what historian Eric Hobsbawn calls a "seismic" social and technological transformation occurred, finally ushering the region into the industrial era. This was the time of Calatrava's youth. The economic, social, and technological revolution that was reshaping the city and the country was accompanied by a change in the collective mentality of the nation.

Calatrava came of age in this extraordinary environment—one that combined a glorious past and abrupt technological change. Walks with his father through the great medieval and Renaissance buildings of Valencia—including the famous structural masterpiece, Lonja del Mercado—reinforced Calatrava's informal education. Upon returning to his rural, secluded village, Calatrava would spend hours obsessively observing nature, drawing, and designing imaginary children's games involving the construction of flying contraptions. The frequent visits to the heaving urban center nearby imparted to Calatrava a strong sense of human affairs and an appreciation of an increasingly formidable modern technology, the flow of time, the force of change, and the power of movement.

Complementing Calatrava's cultural immersion was a formal yet self-directed education that ultimately helped define his unique multidisciplinary approach to architecture. From the age of eight, he attended classes at the Valencia School of Arts and Crafts, where he received special status as an exceptionally talented child. At age fourteen, his mother sent him to Paris to learn French and, at age seventeen, to Zurich to learn German. His travels and the challenge of mastering new languages quickly enriched Calatrava's cultural and design experiences, while simultaneously establishing a sense of independence, self-mastery, and responsibility. He supplemented his high school courses with extracurricular reading that included a descriptive geometry book and, interestingly, a booklet on Le Corbusier. He would assign himself problems from the geometry book and then apply them in an attempt to reproduce the spiral form of the external staircase of Le Corbusier's Unité d'Habitation. It was Ronchamp, however, with its impressive configurational complexity, that would inspire in the young Calatrava even more sophisticated ideas about form, including the interest to discover the secret behind them and the desire to find a method to generate them.

Immediately after completing high school in June 1968, Calatrava enrolled at the Ecole des Beaux-Arts in Paris only to discover the school, students, and city in total upheaval. The social unrest of May 1968 had not only closed the Ecole, but its proponents declared dead the very institutions of art, design, and architecture that Calatrava had come to Paris to embrace. Although sympathetic to the students' causes, Calatrava's revolution would occur through art and architecture, not politics. Returning to Valencia—not out of nostalgia but out of practicality—Calatrava enrolled in both the Architecture School and the Arts and Crafts School. Soon after graduation in 1975, he departed for Zurich to refine his art and architecture training by studying engineering at the Swiss Federal Institute of Technology (ETH). His shift from architecture to engineering's rigorous, abstract, and numerical representation of the world took an even sharper turn during his Ph.D. research.[4]

Begun in 1979 while he was working as an assistant for two construction institutes, Calatrava's thesis, which addressed a complex theoretical problem, was an interdisciplinary study titled On the Foldability of Space Frames (1).[5] The completion of the dissertation in 1981 brought to a close Calatrava's academic training and planted the seeds for his subsequent professional growth and contribution to the discipline of architecture.

01

On the Foldability of Space Frames
ETH, Zurich, Switzerland, 1981

Calatrava's doctoral dissertation followed accepted academic form; it presented a detached exploration of his subject with the intent of producing profound yet abstract knowledge. It intended to systematically generate and enumerate all possible ways that three-dimensional space-frames can be folded first into two dimensions and then into one. Calatrava conceived these abstract geometrical figures to be made as physical objects out of rigid rods linked by movable joints that enabled the entire polyhedron to move, fold, or unfold. As the rods and joints changed position, they traced complex curved lines and surfaces. The important lesson is that the complexity of these resulting bending forms can be generated by a simple mechanism—rods and joints. Yet this simplicity did not mean that the mechanical design of these joints, which allowed the rods to move with a limited degree of freedom, was easily realized. It did suggest, however, a

Facing page
Model partially expanded

01: On the Foldability of Space Frames

powerful system that possessed the potential to show how to pack and unpack structures, and also how to generate a limitless family of curves—a "super-3D compass," or what is called in mathematics a "linkage system," a mechanical instrument for tracing curves, the simplest one being the compass. After the thesis demonstrated that these structures could generate a cornucopia of unprecedented, complex configurations, the untamable forms of Ronchamp could no longer be seen as a puzzle or a scandal, as they were when the building was constructed.

The study, in spite of the apparent analytical dryness of its diagrams and the sternness of its calculations, reveals a passion for real design discoveries. It is driven by a

01: On the Foldability of Space Frames

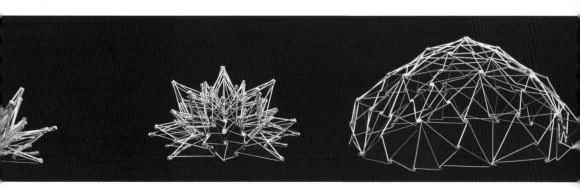

fundamental desire to make any project, and any component of a project (be it construction, conduit, or covering) accommodate waving, drifting, flapping, blowing, or fluttering shapes and to become part of a world in flux, where the capability to change and transform is as important as the capacity to resist forces and introduce stability. Within such a vision, buildings must be able to move and structures must be allowed to extend in all directions and to take any form. This new freedom requires an innovative technological approach that includes new geometries, connections, and mechanisms.

Calatrava's unquenchable fascination with Ronchamp was not centered around the building's voluptuous curves and the controversy sparked by its nebulous function. Nor was he moved to seek notoriety by imitation, an easy accomplishment today thanks to computer modeling technology. Rather, it was the aspiration to discover the thinking behind the forms and the mechanism used to create them, that lured him to the research that resulted in his patented super-compass linkage system.[6]

After completing his thesis in 1981, Calatrava established an architecture and engineering practice, where he could apply his theoretical findings to create a new world of architecture. Even before then, in 1979, he had designed the **Roofing for IBA Squash Hall** (2), a structure intended to be part of a project by Fabio Reinhart and Bruno Reichlin. It is a polemical project that sets the stage for his later work. One part flying machine, one part toy, one part building, this project declared Calatrava's role as engineer–dream-worker, architect-sculptor, and thinker-toymaker,

02
Roofing for IBA Squash Hall
Berlin, Germany, 1979

Facing page
Preliminary sketch (top)
Model of roof structure (bottom)

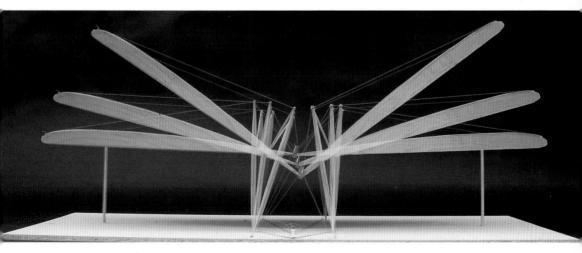

and his commitment to technology, movement, and intellectual challenges.

A large number of the projects presented in this volume are engaged with movement. As already mentioned, they do this in two principle ways: first, through parts of the structure that serve functional needs by *explicitly* moving (unfolding, rising, or revolving, or channeling) objects, people, and vehicles; and second, through parts of the structure that *implicitly* represent movement through their form. In the latter case, the very designs prompt us to reenvision the problem-solving process of the designer. In this respect, Calatrava is simply continuing the age-old mission of architects to attach meaning and a system of beliefs and desires to structures. By the same token, he is also continuing to work within the best rigorist theory. Yet Calatrava also overcomes rigorist dogma and superficiality by giving to the explanation-learning function of design a more profound role, one relevant to our contemporary desires and aspirations. This requires rethinking design to provide a new framework for creating the human-made world: a new poetics of exploring, deciphering, questioning; a system that replaces rigorist reductionism and passive-dogmatic didacticism; a system that operates at the crossroads of problem-solving and design epistemology—in short, a Poetics of Movement.

Calatrava builds this system, aiming toward what we called "optimal" design, the state that maximizes benefits and minimizes costs, pushing his schemes to the outermost limit. Holding the designs within this frontier leads to inefficiency. Pushing them beyond this frontier, this "critical point," leads to collapse. To put it more technically, if a certain variable in design exceeds the "critical point," then the interatomic bonds, the ties between atoms of a structural member, will be broken, and the structure will fly in all directions at once. One must find the narrow place between inefficiency and collapse in order to achieve optimization. Calatrava achieves this "optimal" state on the technical level, while at the same time achieving a powerful aesthetic state that has been called the "pregnant moment." This is an aesthetic concept that refers to a figure of a structure, or sculpture, or even painting, that implies movement. The structure, while totally solid and stationary, forever appears as if in a state of movement, even imminent collapse.

By creating these real and apparent conditions, Calatrava seems to enjoy, like an acrobat or a shrewd dancer, a delight that offers cognitive pleasure—understanding, through metaphors of the body, the order of life and what it means to us as humans. Calatrava's structures arouse wonder, they renew our curiosity, and they engage us in the collective quest to repair the disorder of the world.

Chapter Two
Seminal Projects

Although Calatrava's œuvre is quite diverse and rich, it emerges out of a limited number of basic design strategies that can be traced back to five early projects in which exploration and explanation merge into form. They are the "gene pool" from which many of the ideas and the spatial and structural themes of his later work have originated. Common to all these germinal projects is the imperative to design by solving problems through optimization—that is, minimizing resources and maximizing performance.[1] Calatrava achieves optimization in part by following two major design strategies: profiling elements of a structure, and differentiating elements into specialized function and materials.

Profiling involves defining the contour of a structural member to fulfill Galileo's famous proposition that "it would be a fine thing if one could discover the proper shape to give to an object in order to make it equally resistant at every point."[2] Thus the cross-section of a member changes minutely across that member in order to avoid or minimize the abrupt transfer of forces that can cause structural failure. Planar parts meet in a smooth, continuous, curving fashion, and all parts broaden where they change direction. As a result, the parts are strengthened at their weakest points while allowing their ends to taper gracefully. In fact the ideal silhouette traces the contour of the bending moment diagram and deflection curve. Thus torsion, buckling, and deflection delineate the profile of elements with distended midriffs and minuscule extremities so typical of Calatrava's work.

Differentiation involves dividing a structure into several separate members, each performing a different function, and in each case using the material that best suits the member's assigned function. A structural member that works in both compression and tension is split into two, with the compression member designed in a material suited to that task and the tension member in another. Both members sustain optimal performance in a highly articulated yet integrated body of construction, conduit, and covering parts. Movement pulses through this anatomy. It is explicitly expressed in the configuration of the structure. But it is also tacitly implied by the shape of its fabric.

With each new project that Calatrava designed, discernible patterns of form began to emerge: on one hand, the variation of the cross-sectional profile of a column or beam, accommodating changing forces of loading; on the other, the articulation of individual members in different materials according to structural function.

Two complex structural configuration themes also emerge in these early projects—motifs to be repeated and elaborated in all of Calatrava's later works. One presents an unusual new profile: a leaning, apparently falling column is saved from its fate either by folding the member in the opposite direction to counterbalance the act of falling, resulting in a palindromic figure, or by adding to the column some auxiliary element that either supports or suspends the primary column. The effect is accentuated by concentrating loads to a critical point, slimming sections to a critical extent, and raising the slope lines to a critical degree; structure is thus seen as suspended between stoic permanence and violent disintegration. Between these two states lies the illusion of movement.

Facing page
View of the roof structure of
Jakem Steel Warehouse (3)

03

Jakem Steel Warehouse
Münchwilen, Switzerland, 1983–84

Calatrava's first opportunity to put these ideas to work was the commission to develop a wide-span girder system for the Swiss steel construction company Jakem. This collaboration led to a 1983 commission to expand the Jakem facilities by designing a fourth warehouse in Münchwilen, Switzerland. Although the braced, 10-meter-high post-and-beam structure of the Jakem Steel Warehouse (3) does not contain any unique features, the patented roof system absorbs high loads and distributes them to allow larger openings in the sides of the building. Calatrava's innovative design consists of an identical pair of two-dimensional bow-string trusses that creates a three-dimensional curved upper and a straight bottom girder. Spanning 26 meters, the trusses are joined by struts, stiffened by corrugated sheet metal, and bolted at right angles along their bottom stringers. Forming a triangular frame, the girders taper delicately onto the building's main longitudinal walls to support the continuous surface of the barrel roof and complete the composite design.

To produce optimal results, Calatrava designed arches to act as girders, and as a result obtained efficient performance from the structure. In a similar manner, steel is curved to distribute weight, flattened to brace elements, and corrugated to increase rigidity. Although the upper stringers, due to their curve, are normally in compression from the roof load, the lightweight cladding weighs less than the internal wind pressure. The reversal of loads forces the arches into tension, resting minimally on the triangulated cross beam running the length of the exterior walls. Simpler and lighter to construct than standard trusses—requiring only 28 kilograms of steel per square meter—Calatrava's triangulated girder also demonstrates the latent beauty of the material performing at its best. The Jakem Warehouse is reminiscent of Peter Behren's 1908 AEG Turbine factory in Berlin, yet Calatrava's aesthetic transforms materials; steel takes on the aspect of feathers or leaves to create a thatched roof, for example. Unlike the structural rigorists, Calatrava is not content with the intrinsic beauty of material or of structure and the form it creates.

The principle of optimization pushes structure beyond its traditional applications to achieve an unprecedented truss system. It should be noted, however, that the new system was not achieved in theory only. In collaboration with the client, who was after all the very producer of the construction technology used in the building, Calatrava carried out a number of experiments testing his design proposals. The tests showed that the new roof member was superior to existing ones. It also proved that the Jakem roof had not exhausted its structural possibilities. Thus a new structural type was born, one that provided a point of departure for innovation in Calatrava's work and a reference point for developing his poetics of movement. In keeping with this poetics, a structurally sound solution must also embody virtual movement: the extremes of the configuration and the dynamic outline of the truss do just that. Given our intuition and everyday experiences, we are able, with varying degrees of success, depending on our architectural or physical knowledge, to visualize structures as a potential movement, to trace the forces operating on those structures, and to envision the potential energy trapped within them.

While work was being completed on the Jakem Warehouse, the German casual-wear retailer Ernsting Mini-Laden was planning a new distribution center in Coesfeld, Germany. With the Ernsting Warehouse (4), as with Jakem, Calatrava elevates a project of seemingly limited scope to enhance an industrial image. In this case, however, he explored and expressed untreated, corrugated aluminum to cover the building. Covering an existing concrete frame, each building's facade is an independent yet interdependent event. The focus here is the relation between the envelope of the building, its skin, and its movement: the material covering the 102-meter southern facade appears to ripple in the sun; the loading-bay doors, which measure 10 meters wide, bend in an unprecedented way. Calatrava synthesizes the disparate facades into a holistic image through movement, both explicit and implicit.

The rippled southern facade creates a rhythm of material and light invoking the playful, pulsating waves of light and shadow on the front of ancient Greek temples. The open doors assume the form of a graceful cantilevered roof, with the changes of geometry resembling a gently curving smile that breaks into laughter. Further associations emerge as each of the garage doors folds, rises, and extends like a human limb; when the doors are opened, the "knee" juts forward to provide a kind of protective canopy over the entrance. The canopy's swooping line and the gradual, uniform change of the position of the series of slats—lower at the sides, higher toward the center—provide a simple, functional, and wholly original solution to a potentially graceless technical element. Calatrava went on to patent the solution he created for this warehouse.

04

Ernsting Warehouse

Coesfeld, Germany, 1983–85

Facing page
Detail of south facade

Thus, another new design theme, this one concerning the envelope fabric of the building rather than its construction, was born. No other contemporary building had worked out to such an extent the potentials of envelope and folding. It is a comment, one might say, on Semper's hypothesis that the principle of "dressing," or "Bekleidung," is the true essence of architecture.[3] It is a tantalizing coincidence that Ernsting itself is a firm specializing in textiles and garments.

The Ernsting Warehouse is not only an example of counterintuitive and innovative technical performance. It is also an example of "dream-work": the fundamental transformation of a building's industrial, utilitarian typology to embrace new aesthetic experiences. The doors, or the undulating facing, for example, are more than merely functional; they are a technological metamorphosis of the building's envelope into a metaphor of the clothed body in movement. As metaphorical, anthropomorphic figures, the transformed moving doors smile, wink, bend a knee, raise a gown, disclose both a gaping cavity and unexpected depth, while the facade, as a metaphor of curtain or dress, conceals or reveals the more subtle drama of the building.

As Liane Lefaivre has noted, Calatrava, even with this most industrial vocabulary, practices surrealism in the most rigorous sense of the term.[4] Surrealism, according to Lewis Mumford, reaches the most "willing, wishing, urging passionate part of man's life" that had been "slighted, stifled, and even banished altogether in favor of practical routines."[5] The detection of strong surrealistic elements

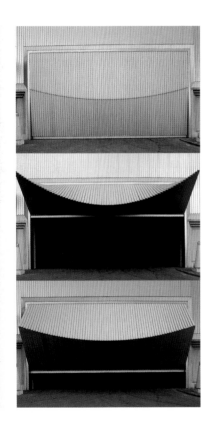

Above
Folding doors in operation

Facing page
View from the road

Above
Corner detail

Facing page
Construction drawings of folding
door mechanism

present in Calatrava's work shows that the poetics of movement developed by him were a design strategy to conceive new forms for skeleton, conduits, and skin, for accommodating not only functional needs, but also psychological and cultural ones.

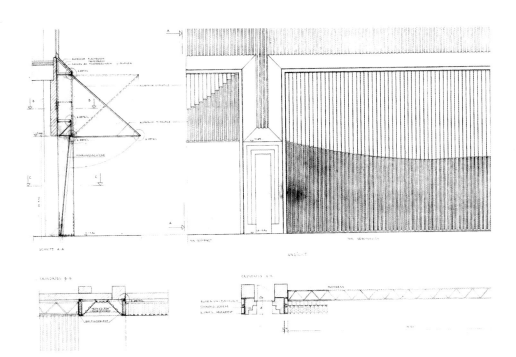

WEST FASSADE

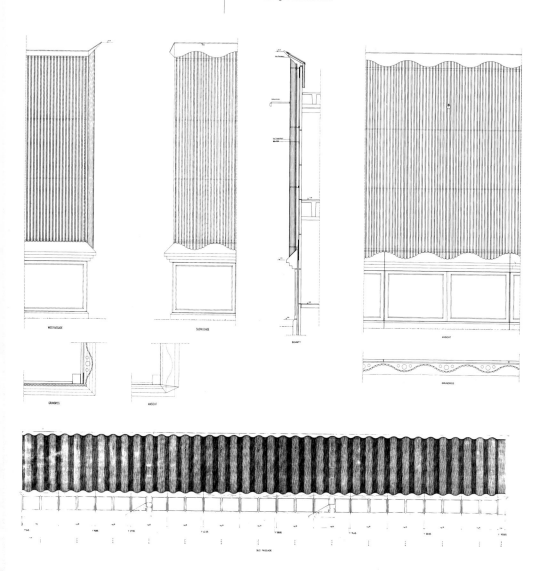

Above
Construction details of wall

Facing page
Two views of the south facade

If the poetics of movement in the Ernsting Warehouse concentrated on the simple metaphors of skin and dress, the **Stadelhofen Railway Station** (5), built from 1983 to 1990, dealt with much more complex aspects of structure, and stymies facile characterization. Since 1945, there have been several fascinating examples of designs for railway stations that relate structure and movement by way of novel spatial arrangements. The Stadelhofen Railway Station in Zurich, a modest project in terms of size, stands apart as probably the most inspired among these buildings. It is an example of an architectural-infrastructure project that brings back the turn-of-the-century romance of travel, bringing together structure and movement.

05

Stadelhofen Railway Station
Zurich, Switzerland, 1983–90

In 1982, the Swiss Federal Railways sponsored a competition to design a new railway station to accommodate a sharp increase in rail traffic. Calatrava won the commission. The highly constrained site, once on the fortified edge of the city and still restricted by a challenging natural topography and an increasingly dense urban conglomeration, appears to have stimulated rather than suppressed the inventiveness of Calatrava's winning design, which drew inspiration from the contours of the surrounding terrain. Rather than build a tunnel, Calatrava, who was then only thirty-two years old, opted to work around and within the old city's fortifications to create a covered promenade, a cantilevered platform roof, and an underground shopping center. Graphically rising alongside 270 meters of track, the promenade consists of a series of 5-meter-long steel pergolas that sweep back from the promenade's edge toward the hill. Four bridges link the upper walkway to the lower platform in punctual intervals that neatly

Facing page
View from above station

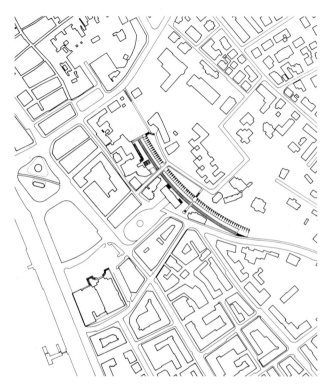

connect the two zones. Underneath, a hollow concrete boxbeam with a convex soffit replaces the original retaining wall, which is supported by an anchored, piled wall in the rear and by a series of slanted, tapering columns in the front. Their outstretched arms carry the additional weight of the walkway above, allowing trains to follow the gentle curve of the hillside. Covering the opposite side of the tracks is a cantilevered roof system. Adjacent to the station, two steel awnings protect travelers entering the subterranean shopping center and close off the entry in the evening. Escalators descend into a series of undulating concrete arches cast in situ at 6-meter intervals.

Above
View of site context (left)
Site plan (right)

Facing page
Station platform

Calatrava referred to this design scheme as "design by section." That was a dissenting statement in the 1980s, when architectural abstract graphics were considered the only way to investigate the spatial qualities of a project, and when the section was perceived as a remnant of a strictly technical way of representing buildings. By contrast, looking at the section drawings for Stadelhofen Railway Station—which accommodate multiple movements and articulate several functional transportation components—one is reminded of complex anatomical section drawings of the human body.

Indeed, the paths and passageways within the station are intertwined like a smooth-flowing circulatory system, directing different types of movement. The highly regulated movement of the trains on the ground level coexists with that of hurried pedestrians ascending and descending the three levels via the stairs and escalators that criss-cross the shopping mall under the tracks. Others cross above them over three pedestrian bridges, while less-harried families and couples enjoy leisurely strolls up and down the hill and along the promenade.

Movement reigns throughout the structure. It can be read in the flow of forces channeled down to the ground via the intricate configurations of steel and ferrovitreous and reinforced concrete. Movement is latent within the profile of columns, beams, cantilevers, platforms, and supporting walls. The retaining wall columns lean back 67 degrees to echo the convex underbelly of the boxbeam. The contour of the cantilevered roof zigzags as if trying to maintain equilibrium, its varying profile adapting to the changing

Above
Construction detail

Facing page
Plan: Level 1 (bottom)
Plan: Level 2 (top)

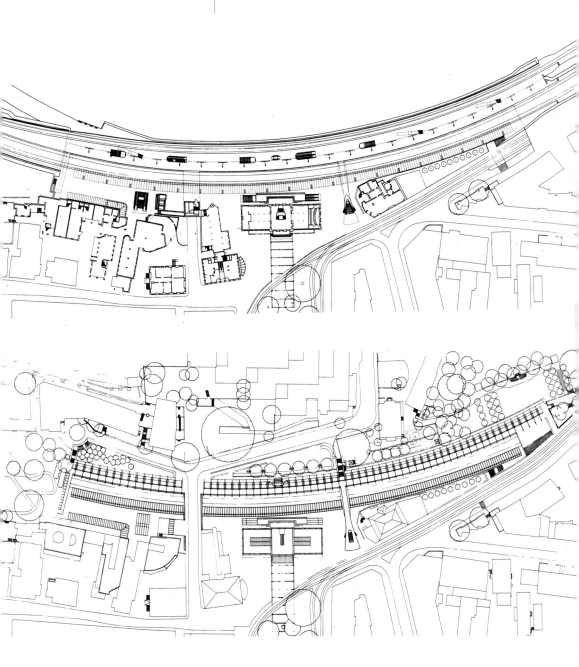

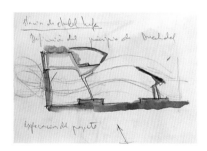

bending moments. As in most Calatrava structures that would follow, the principle of profiling is employed, varying the cross-section of the pergola members to maximize their strength.

Light filters down to the shopping mall through the cantilevered glass-and-metal roof and through the glass blocks of the platform-level sidewalks, while branches and stems of vines move and spread over the cables of the steel pergola that sweeps back from the promenade's edge toward the hill. The zigzag figure and the varying profile of construction members become themes that will be picked up and reworked in later projects.

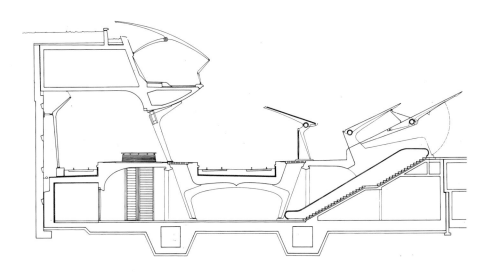

06
Wohlen High School
Wohlen, Switzerland, 1983–88

In 1983, working at the behest of a local architect, Calatrava used differentiation to explore the themes of coverage and enclosure in the roofing of four public spaces in the Wohlen High School (6) in Switzerland. As in the case of the Jakem and Ernsting warehouses, which ultimately resulted in flamboyant configurations, Calatrava was asked to do a relatively modest job: add to and improve an existing structure. Calatrava, however, saw in this commission—as he had in the earlier ones—the opportunity to experiment, test, demonstrate new ideas, and develop his poetics of movement. Thus for each area of the building, which had a unique function and a distinct location within the larger site, he responded by applying a different construction system, different materials, and different configurations for the structural members.

A 5-meter arched entry canopy bridges the two converging wings of the school. Its spine is a tubular arch, out of which a series of riblike members are cantilevered. The arch stretches obliquely to the surface of the facade like the wing of a bird, and protects the students who pass under it. Once inside, visitors are greeted by a radial space, 11.4 meters wide, that invokes the form of a flower. Retained by a steel tension ring, twenty 5.4-meter-long hollowed segments carry roof loads to the central compression ring. Hovering above this steel flower is a 2-meter-wide glazed roof lantern. Opaque glass sheathes a series of radially arranged laminated-wood girders, cables, and steel spindles, specifically designed to manifest the flow of the forces through them. The resulting pattern provides a key public meeting point for students and unifies an otherwise disjointed space, thereby placing

This page
The glazed roof lantern of the
entry hall

Facing page
The irregularly vaulted library,
with its single, central column

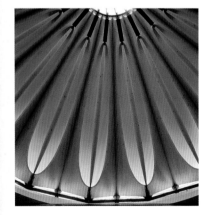

structure at the service of architecture to create a memorable aesthetic effect of orientation and identity.

Beyond the entry hall, the library presents the structural
properties of a thin concrete shell. Covering a two-story
space, four unequal vaults descend hyperbolically to a single point. (Once again, Calatrava encouraged metaphors
that did not necessarily relate to the structural performance of the components: he referred to the scheme's
configuration as an open book, or a bird with stretched
wings.) Rising 4 meters, a radially reinforced steel column
carries the entire roof load and serves as the drainpipe for
cascading rainwater. Almost completely detached from the
side walls, discreetly placed steel spindles stabilize the

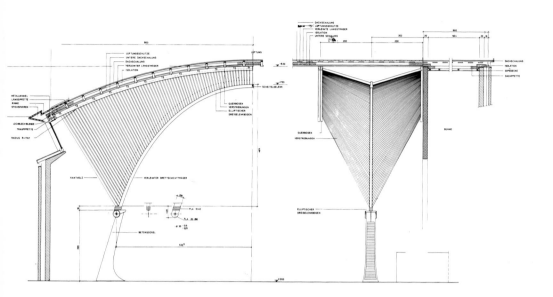

shell. As natural light flows into the building, illuminating the interior, an illusion of floating is created, accentuating the relationship between the ceiling's surface and the solitary column. Adjacent to the library are five prefabricated, three-pin parabolic arches covering a 16-by-28-meter assembly hall. Their deep triangular sections, consisting of individual pine battens, flow upward to support the roof, which, distinct from the exterior walls, allows natural light to pour into the hall.

With the Wohlen High School project, the design strategies of optimizing through profiling and differentiation served once more to solve the classic problem of roof support. For the entry hall Calatrava used wood for tensile

Above
Section and structural details

Facing page
Assembly hall

members, constricting the opening of the sculpted triangular arch section. Tilted to continue the cant of the arch and widened at the end to take lateral loads, the assembly hall columns reveal their dominant forces. The cantilevered arch fuses structure and circulation. It identifies and encloses the entrance. Articulation of the entry hall maximizes coverage and minimizes material, creating a lighter structure with a greater span to demarcate the space below. The ribs and columns of the assembly hall provide a scale the roof structure alone cannot establish. By allowing forces to define form, Calatrava's innovations emerge from known precedents—the column, the arch, the roof, all of which are apparently "timeless" architectural elements. We discover that it is the principles shaping form, rather than the token shapes themselves, that are timeless.

These buildings or building complexes that Calatrava designed at an early stage of his career contained significant ideas for the development of the rest of his work, but he was developing other ideas in his designs for other types of structures. During the same period as the design of buildings already described, Calatrava designed and constructed the Bach de Roda bridge. A bridge is, at its most basic, a spanning structure. From this point of view it is not different from any other structure spanning an opening, such as those for the roofs of Wohlen High School or the Jakem Steel Warehouse. Spanning structures such as roofs and arches, however, merely cover and protect; they do not address or alter the specific patterns of circulation that occur under them. Bridges, on the other hand, are by their very definition intended to provide passage and restore communication. They are specialized

Facing page
Roof of assembly hall

Facing page
Bridge cabling system

Below
Preliminary sketches

07

Bach de Roda Bridge

Barcelona, Spain, 1984–87

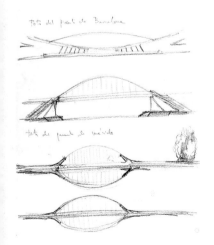

to *accommodate* human circulation. Structure and movement are united into one object.

For the Bach de Roda Bridge (7), Calatrava employed the same design strategies of differentiation and profile to create an enormous spanning structural element that would serve as a conduit for pedestrian, automobile, and train movement. Conceived in 1984, after Barcelona's bid to host the 1992 Olympic Games was accepted, the bridge traverses the embankments of a railway station to connect the area of Sant Andrea to San Marti, creating in the process one of the most expansive public parks in Barcelona. Built between 1986 and 1987, its 129-meter concrete deck hovers 8 meters over park and railway. Interior arches support a 46-meter span, reinforced against buckling by an exterior arch that carries an additional pedestrian walkway and access stairs. Streamlined reinforced-concrete pylons support the main arches at the edge of the traffic lanes. Canted against these main arches are secondary, steel stiffening arches, supported by attenuated abutments. The stairs, which grant access to parks on either side, follow the profile of these abutments up to the pedestrian areas, which widen into the form of a bow between each pair of steel arches.

Calatrava rethought a classic bridge design by relinquishing traditional structural paradigms. The common approach to the problem of arch-buckling is to laterally brace arch pairs via interconnecting trusses. Calatrava's solution, however, is to place next to the main arches secondary arches of equal height, which lean inward and are connected by fins that brace both arches against

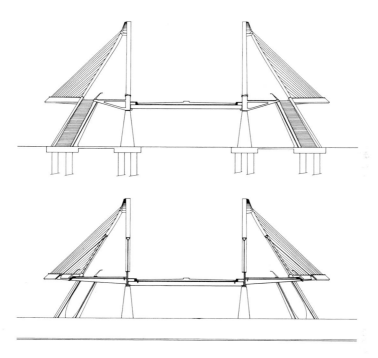

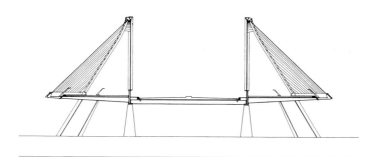

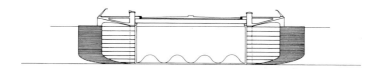

This page
Sections

Facing page
Night view

buckling. This solution eliminates the need to place a bracing truss between the two main arches. Once more, we can see Calatrava's multipurpose, fusing, and reconciling approach. The scheme serves simultaneously many diverse needs and requests. The solution is successful in terms of both construction and culture. The configuration of main and secondary arches and suspension cables helps to identify a location distinct from the roadway and to create a landmark in place of just an anonymous route. The supporting arch curves to the ground gracefully to create a stairway for access to the bridge piazza. The resulting continuity of form, as in most Calatrava structures, minimizes the abrupt transfer of forces. But at the same time, it results in visual congruity between the leisurely flow of pedestrians mounting the bridge and the more rushed pace of vehicles streaming across it.

By encompassing multifaceted movement in a single static form, the bridge becomes nexus for person, car, and train. The division of labor within the structure of the arches collaborates with the differentiated flow of human and mechanical movement. Disparate subsystems coexist—at once independent and interdependent.

More than just a practical tool, the bridge thus emerges as a means par excellence to heal the wounds wrought by the usually brute-force technological invasion of rail and automobile traffic. In this spirit, the Bach de Roda bridge tries to restore both the physical and symbolic connections that sustain a disrupted community; at the same time it offers a striking urban monument and a human-scale landmark to an otherwise diffuse and fragmented urban landscape.

Together with the other seminal projects examined in this
chapter, the Bach de Roda bridge established precedents
and generated a recognizable "Calatrava style" that fuses
aesthetic "sculptural style" with engineering's "solution
style." It is with these defining structures that Calatrava
reveals the deeper, cognitive approach to design and
reality that will become the hallmark of his work.

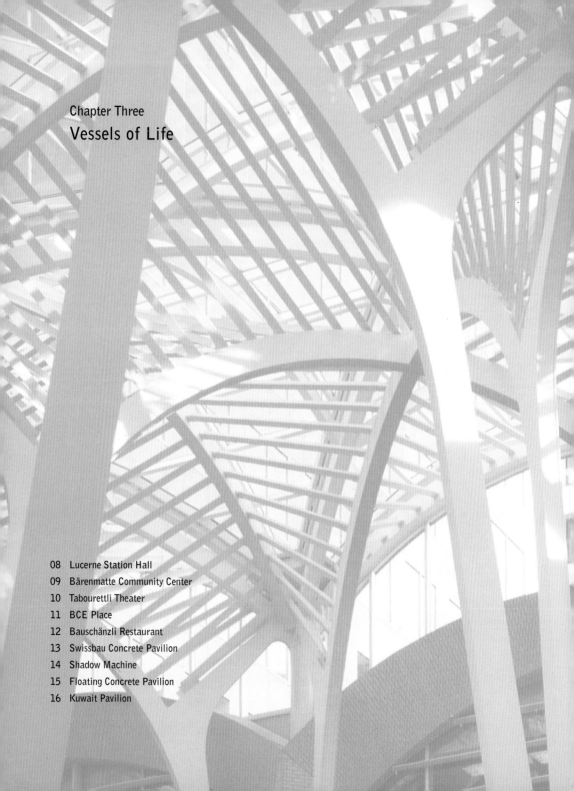

Chapter Three
Vessels of Life

From the mid-1980s Calatrava began to explore and exploit the themes first developed in the seminal projects of his early career. These were projects that primarily concerned enclosure and the traditional architectural qualities of space, entry, covering, and light. They addressed the ageless problem of architecture: to contain, cover, and protect by developing an efficient structure and envelope. For Calatrava, however, equal priority is always given to the objective of movement. In the following projects, a higher order of complexity is developed. Circulation conduits are interwoven, integrated, or incorporated within the structural components themselves. Movement, both explicit and implied, redefines, reconfigures, and revives static form and, ultimately, the long-standing norms of structural elements and building types.

The first of this new, more complex generation of projects was the **Lucerne Station Hall** (8), an addition to the original 1896 building and to its 1975 modification. The project uses the Stadelhofen Railway Station columnar motif, as well as the now familiar strategies of optimizing structure through differentiation and profiling, all of which are highly evident in the most distinguished element of the project—the portico. We see here the same balancing act of configuration, the same specialized devices acting in compression and tension to keep the structure stable, the same effect of apparent movement. The motif is carried here to a gigantic, imposing, excessive scale reminiscent of a Renaissance colonnade of the so-called giant or colossal order. The monumentality of the sixteen 14-meter-high columnar elements and their compression columns stands as testament to the complex movement within and around the sublevel concourse area it envelops. Forming an arcade for cyclists, canted columns carry the horizontal thrust of the glazed facade. Above, the first concrete portico braces the individual units while enclosing the space below. The differentiated and architecturally viable three-dimensional support system for the curtain wall enabled Calatrava to perch a 109-meter-long cantilevered portico as a counter-weight to a suspended glass roof. Rising 19 meters high, wire cables run from the portico's interior edge to penetrate the glass roof at the central anchor point of the metal trusses. This triangular tensile system supports the light steel beams and glass roof that are suspended over the lower portico. This delicate balancing act allows Calatrava to avoid a major intrusion into the complex by establishing a virtually freestanding hall appended along the length of the station's facade. Although the hall is a distinctive and independent volume, it does not exceed the height of the adjacent buildings, so its proportions are in harmony with those of the neighboring neoclassical buildings. In this way, Calatrava has woven the site, the surrounding structures, and his design solution into a synthesis of engineering and architecture.

Facing page
View of the station and its concrete portico

09

Bärenmatte Community Center

Suhr, Switzerland, 1984–88

Extrapolating from the unique roof profile of the Jakem Steel Warehouse to achieve a heightened sense of differentiation, Calatrava began to work in 1984 on the concert hall of the **Bärenmatte Community Center** (9) in Switzerland. As with the Lucerne Station Hall, the commission called for the completion and renovation of an existing structure. Calatrava, however, redefined and transformed the previous work by once again completely exploiting his original themes. The design spans the stipulated 25-meter-length of the hall by combining tensile and compressive forces. Calatrava reduced the original triangular girder to a V-shaped compression arch and a trio of tensile cables. The cascading, 7.2-meter-high apex of the parabolic arch dictates the level of the exterior roofing. The outward horizontal elements at the base of each arch are connected by tension cables. The sleek, chromium-plated steel cables nestle within the beams to transform the ceiling into what appears to be a stringed instrument. Skylights span the hall's length, admitting abundant natural light that is then diffused by the gaps between the arches and the cable penetrations. Below the cable ties, a deeper, triangular section resists a bending moment and transfers vertical loads to 2.6-meter-high steel vertical T-sections, rhythmically defining the building's outer walls. By spanning the interior space without secondary supports, Calatrava imbues the hall with versatility, the chief requirement of a multipurpose community center. In addition, he introduces elements of a human scale to aid the visitor in comprehending the vast space. The aluminum-clad foyer doors form a soundproof surface, with their triangular tops flush against the sloping soffit. When opened, the doors reveal additional soffit light fixtures, elegantly marking the transition from foyer to grand performance hall.

Facing page
Detail of ceiling fixture in the performance hall

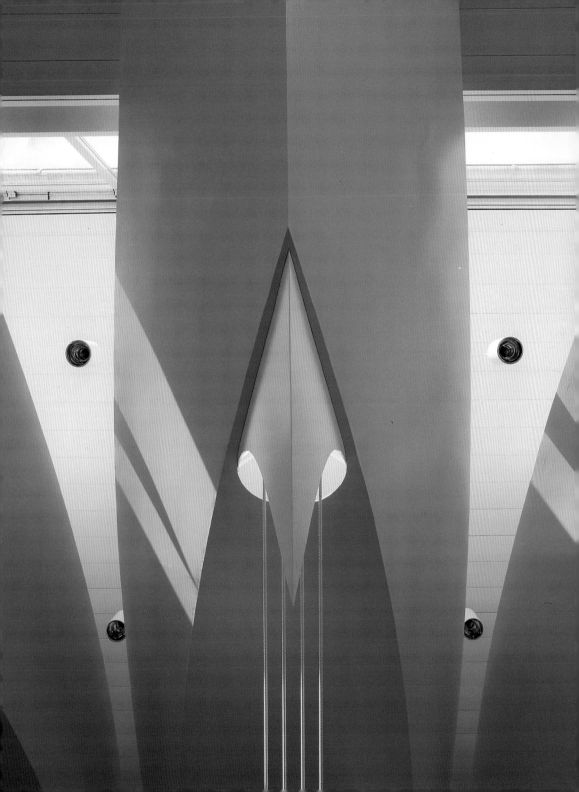

Above and facing page
Aluminum-clad foyer doors

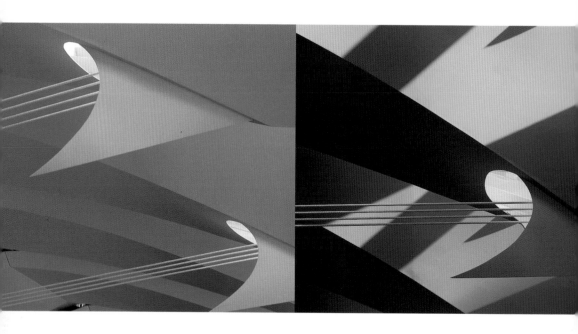

Above
Details of light fixtures and
tension cables

Facing page
Performance hall

10

Tabourettli Theater

Basel, Switzerland, 1986–87

In yet another remodeling commission, this time in the heart of Basel, Switzerland, Calatrava was asked to renovate the **Tabourettli Theater** (10) in 1986. The theater is a medieval building that since the 1970s has housed two cabaret theaters. In 1984, the top floor and roof space had been designated to become apartments. For this project, Calatrava once again elaborated on the roof structure–spanning theme developed for Jakem. The building's existing structure was problematic: due to the removal of three supports to create an unobstructed theater space, the main timber beam in the center of the building had sunk. Calatrava proposed using the roof structure to suspend the 211-ton ceiling load. Steel tension rods running through the upper floor's partition walls connect to a braced, triangulated structure in the roof. With the roof carrying the central load, the ceiling joists below can span the entire length of the theater. The reduced load on the rest of the structure also minimizes the dimensions of the interior beams and offers Calatrava an opportunity to assign them an acoustical function as well. The elements Calatrava created within the cabaret are multifaceted mobile machines: the auditorium entrance revolves, window shutters fold upward, the dressing room features an octagonal, transformational box, and the bar transforms into a miniature stage set.

The Tabourettli, however, also had problems from below: the theater's floor required further support. Rather than radically altering the building's ancient structure to make it stronger, Calatrava inserted a steel trestle, which interlocks with the new stair, to divert the forces and brace the weakening longitudinal beams of the ground and first

Facing page
View of stairway, looking down

floors. Interweaving the trestle and stairs infused a sense of new vitality into the old structure. By concentrating the building's first-floor beam loads into a single unit, this solution avoids the potential shortcomings of the ancient structural members and the inadequate peripheral foundations. Above, a pair of webbed elements transfer a portion of the ceiling load to the inclined steel members. In addition, the stair and steel-framed glass bridge spanning the double-height space of the theater serve as both circulation paths and structural elements. By avoiding the need to insert heavy load-bearing members, Calatrava provided ample space for the cloakroom, the ticket counter, the public facilities, and the main entry on the ground floor.

As a functional and modern counterpoint to the ancient framework, Calatrava's solution physically and figuratively resuscitates the building. Yet its real strength lies in redefining the structural forces of the existing building. The ceiling becomes the main structural element, joining the roof 5 meters above it and the masonry walls. The staircase that floats above the floor transfers weight away from the foundation to a centrally located basement support. Both interventions create a new potential in the existing building to arrive at a complementary and integrated structural solution.

Perhaps the most important development in the project is the strategy of differentiation of the spanning structure. Similar to organic development, where tissue gradually specializes to perform a discrete function, the dictates of compression, tension, and torsion lead Calatrava to isolate each type of force in elements designed to optimize the material performance. Calatrava's use of differentiation

Facing page
View of steel stair-trestle

reached new heights in this design. Like an orchestra, which combines totally disparate instruments to create harmony, the building uses separate elements to generate a collaborative, interdependent system.

In the cabaret ceiling, differentiation, as interpreted by Calatrava, leads to tensile wood baffles that complement the chromium metal compression members like the bottom chord in a triangular beam section. The trestle columns optimize material by strategically placing more load toward the center to counter column buckling, while their wider feet resist increased torsion and subsequent rotation. The resulting configuration is a counterpoint to the standard column, improving the material performance to resist the inherent forces within columns. The same design strategy, the same profiling and geometries that we

Above
Cabaret with folding window shutters

Facing page
Dressing room with transformable octagonal box

find in large-scale structural elements are carried through to
even the smallest scale, in elements such as chairs and tables.
Calatrava's poetics of movement achieve a spatial sense of
order and morphological unity that rival those found in classical building and furniture. The profile of each element fluctu-
ates according to the forces it carries.

Celebrating the wonderful relationship between compression
and tension and expressing the hidden forces within elements
requires a flexible approach to material and an agility of mind.
Calatrava's rigorous understanding of both existing systems and
structural precedents enables him to work through their inherent structural constraints to innovate appropriately and with
formal sensitivity. By applying the same principles to a universe
of objects of different size and usage, Calatrava creates a thor-
oughly integrated world, a *gesamtkunstwerk*, or total work of art.

In 1987, Calatrava was among a group of designers invited to submit proposals for a mixed-use complex called **BCE Place** (11) in the teeming core of downtown Toronto. The complex was to include shops, restaurants, and other leisure outlets. Calatrava went beyond the original programmatic brief to propose a towering gallery enclosing the entire 130-meter area of the broad city block. Unlike the arcades of nineteenth-century Europe, Calatrava's gallery is an independent structure imposing a new order among disparate buildings.

Eight inwardly inclined steel supports bifurcate upward, eventually meeting to form pointed parabolic vaults spanning 14 meters across the interior space. As architectural elements, they simultaneously establish a rhythmic colonnade at the street level and an undulating glazed roof 27 meters above. Near the center of the arcade, there is a dramatic interruption of this structure. Over a 30-by-3-meter regular plan, treelike structures rise and support nine intersecting barrel vaults, creating a "forest" effect. The glazed, translucent roof envelops the square below with wide, upturned parabolas. Below, in the center, is a circular fountain of steel tubes, opening like a flower.

As a building type, the BCE fuses the neo-Victorian arcade with the more modern, urbanistic idea of inserting a garden between the buildings in a central business district. Behind the neo-Victorian precedents are even older models, namely that of the Gothic cathedral's nave and aisle. Rather than resorting to the imitation of these precedents, however, Calatrava reinterprets them as "forests" of structural "trees."

11
BCE Place
Toronto, Canada, 1987–92

Facing page
Canopy roof between buildings

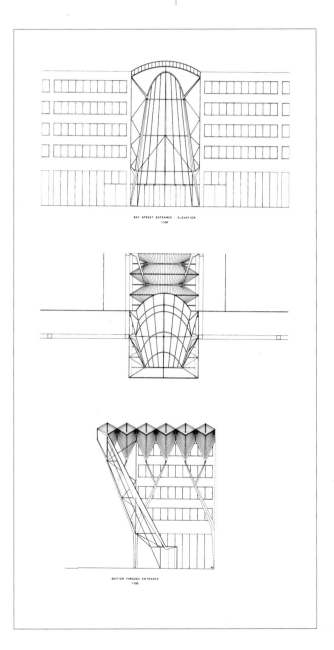

BAY STREET ENTRANCE · ELEVATION
1:100

SECTION THROUGH ENTRANCE
1:100

This page
Drawings of entrance (left)
View through the gallery (below)

Facing page
View of site context

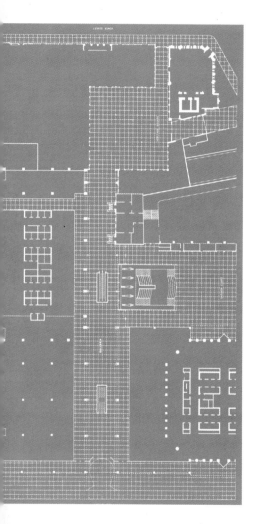
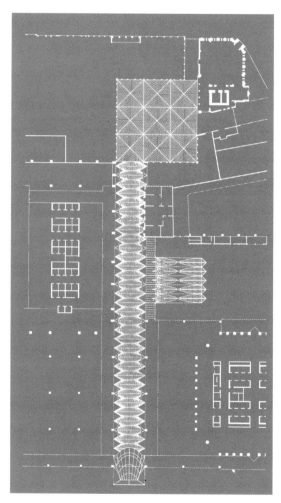

Above
Plans

Facing page
View of garden plaza

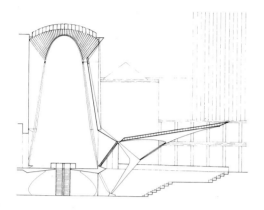

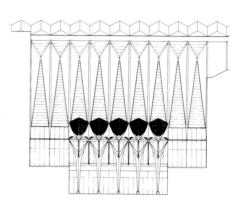

Above
Sections

Facing page
Detail of roof structure

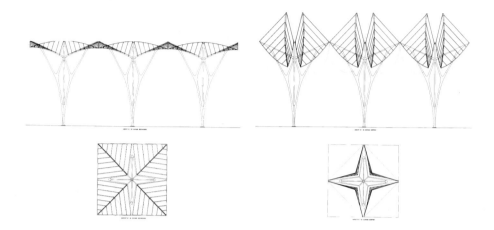

12
Bauschänzli Restaurant
Zurich, Switzerland, 1988

Calatrava explored the tree structure metaphor even further with the open-air **Bauschänzli Restaurant** (12), situated near a medieval fortress on an island in Zurich's Limmat River. Calatrava proposed to implant nine metal-and-glass structures, each 12 meters high, amid natural trees. Each of these structures is topped by a mechanically operated, foldable roof composed of four interlocking, glazed panels, hinging upward along eight edges in a star pattern. Unfolded, the inclining planes create a continuous canopy to enclose the restaurant in inclement weather; when retracted, they uncover the restaurant. The roofs blur the distinction between structure and architecture by exploiting the dynamic nature of enclosure through movement. Accessible by a small footbridge, the space is further refined by Calatrava's decision to submerge the services and restaurant kitchen.

Above
Drawings of roof canopy in
opened and closed positions

Facing page
Model of roof canopy

This page
Sketch (top)
Detail of concrete pivots (bottom)

Facing page
Concrete "fingers"

13

Swissbau Concrete Pavilion

Basel, Switzerland, 1989

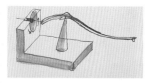

For the 1988 Swiss Building Fair in Basel, the Swiss Association of Manufacturers of Precast Concrete Elements asked Calatrava to develop a structure to demonstrate modern concrete-casting technology. This commission for the Swissbau Concrete Pavilion (13) allowed Calatrava to refine his previous experiments to focus on the extreme possibilities of prefabrication in concrete.

Conceptually, the pavilion shows how, through movement, static forms can be related to nature. Literally, it is a machine of concrete, able to change its own shape through the coordinated yet distinct movements of its elements. Through harmonic periodicity, the normally rigid material is set in motion to challenge the image of concrete as an inert, motionless construction material.

Calatrava refined his polemic by issuing a challenge to the manufacturers themselves. To impart a smooth, refined finish to each of the fourteen 7.8-meter-long concrete "fingers" required an oiled, linoleum-lined, compound-curve formwork; precise consideration of internal steel reinforcement; and meticulous temperature control during the curing process. Weighing 1.2 tons and tapering from 52 to 10 centimeters in width, each individual finger cantilevers 1.86 meters out from the rear support wall, balancing on concrete pivots. Each element can be moved via a crank connecting the "knuckles" to a row of elliptical pins mounted on rotating disks. The volumes, patterns, and undulating enclosure trace a movement that suggests a waving hand.

14

Shadow Machine

New York, New York,
and Venice, Italy, 1992–93

Similar to the desirable ambiguity emerging in the Swissbau Pavilion, Calatrava's **Shadow Machine** (14) more force-
fully enters into the nebulous region between science and
art, exploring the shadowy boundaries between sculpture
and architecture. For Calatrava, sculpture is an embarka-
tion point from which to seek new vistas of these in-
between worlds. At the 1992 exhibition devoted to his
work, mounted by the Museum of Modern Art in New
York, Calatrava inaugurated his laboratory for the public.
Commissioned specifically for this one-man show, the
Shadow Machine represents the continuation of Calatrava's
kinetic sculpture research, begun in 1988 for the Swissbau
Pavilion. In this iteration, the molded precast concrete fingers are longer and lighter than their early counterparts.
Eight meters long and weighing 600 kilograms, each of the
twelve elements rests on the end of fixed supports pro-
truding from a 30-ton base. Cast-in sockets support and
enable flexibility of the tapered end, which is connected to
an automated ball within the base. Powered by mounted
drives on the rear support panel, the fingers move inde-
pendently. Similar to the Swissbau Pavilion project, the
machine produces a perpetual, staggered, synchronized
motion, progressively changing the angle of engagement.
The movement is dynamic; a direct connection between
the finger and the drive socket transmits the full circular
motion of the drive out to the tips, creating variable patterns and shadows on the space below.

As a sculpture, the *Shadow Machine* is a deceptively simple
device. Its childlike play belies the complex forces at
work in this moving laboratory. Calatrava is pursuing a
profound research agenda, bringing to life the clandestine

Facing page
Shadow Machine at the Museum
of Modern Art, New York

relationship between structure and architecture. Via movement, architectural exploration and structural investigation merge and transform into experience: a concrete machine changes shape by the coordinated movements of its elements. Through light modulation, shadow patterns continuously change. Whereas Calatrava's previous buildings allowed light to flow through them to increase illumination, here the structure actively creates shadows. The opening and closing of the rooflike structure undermines assumptions about rigid height, span, and coverage. The asymmetrical movement of the individual members reconfigures the interconnection and coordination of compositional elements—when each has a life of its own, the unit as a whole creates new, unforeseen forms.

The *Shadow Machine* is an abstract exercise in how movement can give elements a greater flexibility. Movement from one physical state to another indicates the potential variations of adaptation, endowing form with the ability to change in response to its environment, use, and structural forces. This potential to adapt to changing needs and contexts is within the structure itself, not in the relation to its individual parts. Since the elements do not move in a uniform manner, the machine avoids simple up-and-down motion to continually create new theoretical surfaces. Increasing responsiveness to changing needs occurs by facilitating change through an intelligence of the parts. With movement, the artificial world of concrete is directly related to the adaptability and flexibility inherent in the natural world. The work is a manifesto: movement is a precondition for adaptive form. Yet it is also a polemic in defense of dream-work. The Swissbau Concrete Pavilion,

Above
Transporting Icaros in Venice

Facing page
Icaros installed in Venice

the *Shadow Machine,* and a similar piece called *Icaros,* exhibited in Venice, all generate a dreamlike effect caused by the aimlessness with which the structures seem to move. They each impel concrete to perform in a manner contrary to expectations, with a fluidity of movement normally associated with other materials. Each piece generates oneiric tension and excitement and creates associations with the act of flying. Indeed, flying is a common theme in dreams.

No matter how many times we experience the slow, perpetual, hypnotic movement of these machines, we are left with a strange and unreal feeling enhanced by the rhythmic modulations of light and shadow. Concrete, categorized as a hard and heavy material, is suddenly engaged in light and graceful movement. It is at once a wholly unprecedented yet strangely familiar sight. The smoothness of the surface and the geometry of the curves of the concrete pieces are strongly reminiscent of the marble elements of classical architecture. The very movement of the elements recall those of a large bird, or a dolphin, or the hands of a dancer.

The *Shadow Machine* shows the extreme possibilities of prefabrication in concrete; it is a sculptural experiment, a "microworld," that explores the relationship between structure and movement, between rational inquiry and dream, and between conventionality and freedom. The results of this exploration are fed into Calatrava's later designs of mobile roofs of buildings, demonstrating the creative symbiosis between sculpture and engineering in the œuvre of Calatrava.

14: Shadow Machine

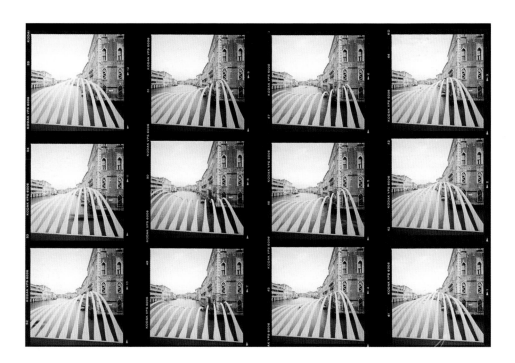

Above
Icaros in motion

Facing page
View of Icaros mechanism

In preparation for the 700th anniversary of the Swiss Emancipation, in 1991, Calatrava conceived a maneuverable **Floating Concrete Pavilion** (15). This was an opportunity to incorporate the abstract spatio-structural movement of the *Shadow Machine* into a new functional form—the budding dome. The budding dome is a mechanically operated roof whose parts open and close very much like a flower. The mobile, fingerlike elements of the previous two experiments become densely ordered cantilevered roof ribs that fold into a dome and open out to create an interior open-air space.

Forming a 600-square-meter floating platform in the Lake of Lucerne, the facility can be used as an auditorium, as an exhibition space, or even as a means of transportation. The pavilion provides an unmistakable landmark whose configuration can change due to the raising and lowering of twenty-four leaflike structural members. Representing the twenty-four cantons of Switzerland, the radially arranged precast concrete armatures open by pivoting on trunnion pins set into twenty-four inclined ribs.

15
Floating Concrete Pavilion
Lucerne, Switzerland, 1989

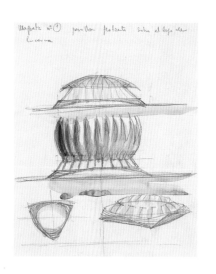

Each of the 12-meter-high columns, placed 3.3 meters apart, support a steel compression ring 30 meters in diameter. They rest on a buoyant, triangular substructure divided into twenty-four air-tight compartments housing technical services. The blossoming concentric pattern of concrete establishes a dialogue with one of the most picturesque mountain- and waterscapes in central Switzerland. Accordingly, it is the flexibility and transformative power of nature that Calatrava imbues into his architecture.

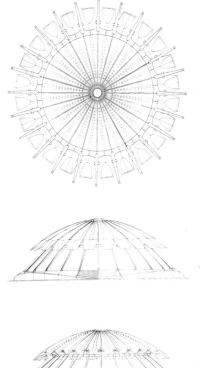

Above
View of the mechanically operating
roof or budding dome (left)
Plan (top right)
Elevation (middle right)
Section (bottom right)

16
Kuwait Pavilion
Seville, Spain, 1991–92

Shortly after the 1990–91 Gulf War, Calatrava created a multifaceted, symbolic structure called Kuwait Pavilion (16), which was commissioned at the behest of the emirate for the 1992 World's Fair in Seville, Spain. The roof structure is a hybrid of the budding dome design scheme of the Floating Concrete Pavilion and the *Shadow Machine*. The roof is another dome made up of mobile elements, but the elements come together not like the petals of a flower, but like the long, tapered fingers of two hands, or perhaps more appropriately in the present case, like the leaves of two palm branches. Seventeen 25-meter-long finger-elements, constructed in timber and supported by hydraulically operated reinforced-concrete columns, interlock to form an impenetrable vault and then unfold to reveal the gentle barrel-shape of the 525-square-meter piazza. The piazza is glazed with panels of laminated structural glass and translucent marble that illuminate the gallery below during the day and glow with an enigmatic inner light at night when uncovered. When half closed, the roof casts light and shadow on the piazza below, providing protection from the sun, like a palm-shaded oasis.

Surrounding the piazza are two concave walls and two rows of equidistant concrete pillars that lean toward each other. Defying the dichotomies of structure and sculpture, strong associations emerge: a row of sabers, raised in the air, saluting, facing each other in a splayed defensive pose, and yet cooperating to support opposing blades. However, the forms suggest a captivating moral to a fable rather than any programmatic "message," such as those embedded in the designs of national pavilions in the past. The wide base

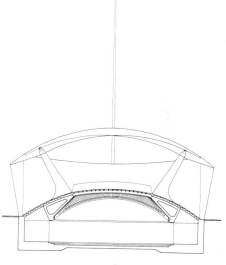

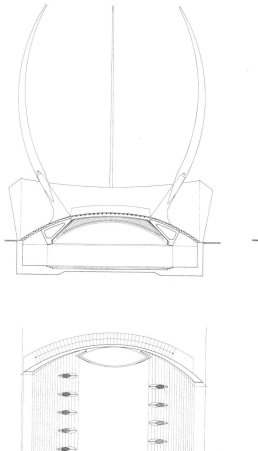

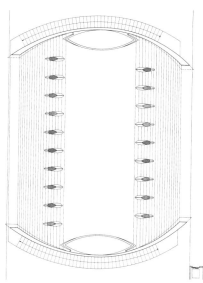

Facing page
Roof structure opened

This page
Sections with roof open (top left)
and closed (top right)
Plan (bottom)

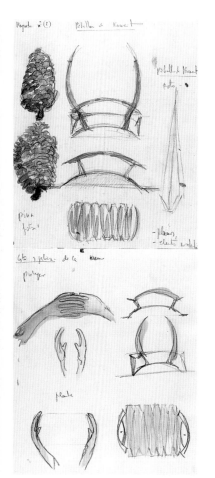

of the pillars eliminates traditional Western architectural categories that distinguish between exterior and interior spaces, and certainly between objects of sculpture and structure.

The enigmas above ground in the Kuwait project are mere hints of the permanent exhibition space below. Descending along the convex edge of the end walls eventually reveals the structure beneath the gently bulging form of the piazza. Reminiscent of the exterior fingers in form and material, arched triangular trusses emerge from beams running the length of the space. As with the exterior, lightness is emphasized by the material differences between timber latticework and reinforced concrete. These arches span 14 meters over the main exhibition area, which is finished in black marble. Three steps further lies a peripheral area, treated with white marble. By day the exhibition area is indirectly lit by a calm sheen of natural light filtering through the translucent laminated ceiling. Additionally, triangular slits in the piazza staircase light the peripheral areas. By night, the flow of light is reversed, with the light sources in the subterranean space illuminating the piazza above.

The sense of oneiric spatial continuity characterizes the uncommon relationship between the two worlds, above and below, of the Kuwait Pavilion. The mobility of the roof allows interpretations of the building as either a piazza with a roof or a court with high walls and offers benefits of functional flexibility. At the same time, the movement of artificial palm branches, closing and opening, suggests engineering sagacity combined with sculptural clairvoyance.

Above
Detail view of roof from below

Facing page
Preliminary sketches

Below
Study for a structure

Facing page
Detail of roof in motion

The intimate relationship between the upper and lower world of the Kuwait Pavilion gives birth to a new kind of space. The roof becomes optional: when the palm branches are closed, the piazza gains a roof structure; when open to the sky, high, soaring walls suddenly appear to engulf the visitors. The only clear architectural features—concave walls with tangible thickness and weight—just serve to emphasize the lightness and structural dynamics of the roof. The graceful lean of the structural colonnade supports the flexible roof structure while simultaneously giving the piazza a porous edge. Echoing the structure and architectural synthesis above, the chamber of the piazza imbues architectural structure with new meaning. Within the subterranean gallery, Calatrava invokes the lightness of the piazza by deploying similar materials and compositional elements.

Calatrava's projects serve, use, and explore the transformational power of movement. Borders between people, space, and institutions dissolve to reemerge transformed: recombined, rethought, and reborn. The consequent agenda of polemics and the poetics of movement is to embrace the daily metamorphosis of place—its natural, environmental, cultural, and social changes.

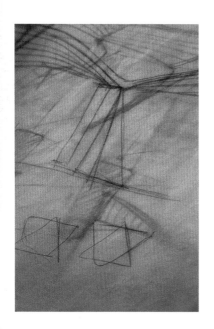

Chapter Four
Bridges for Community

A bridge is a complex artifact. It is structure and conduit combined. Bridges rise over natural disruptions of movement as well as man-made hindrances to circulation and interaction. They are intended to restore communication and community. Perhaps no other human artifact better represents the human need for and commitment to continuity, life, and change.

Calatrava's syncretic design approach fits the synthetic qualities of the bridge. His strategies of optimization of efficiency through differentiation and profiling, which had been developed in the earlier, seminal projects, evolve further by focusing on the configuration of the various spanning components of bridges. Calatrava's bridge designs revisit and reconceptualize classic typologies. At the same time, their innovative linking elements become literally the intellectual bridges between divided territories. Engineering grows into sculpture, and sculpture incorporates engineering. The artifact embraces the environment—and thus succeeds in meeting the challenge posed to postwar architects and engineers by Le Corbusier's Ronchamp. The result is a symbiotic catalyst that enhances the landscape and upgrades the quality of the local urban life.

The Alamillo Bridge (17), completed in just thirty-one months for the 1992 World's Fair in Seville, Spain, was instantly recognized as a landmark, joining the list of numerous memorable historic structures in this remarkable city. The bridge was a response to the needs of Andalusian officials, who sought to improve the connections between Seville and the neighboring towns. To span two river crossings, Calatrava initially proposed two

visually interrelated bridges. The combined effect of the
two structures would have been an unprecedented design
paragon: a veritable megasculpture, implanted in the landscape, consisting of a pair of symmetrically inclined 142-
meter-high pylons, approximately 1.5 kilometers apart and
connected by the Puenta de la Cartuja Viaduct. The massive tilted pylons implied movement. They suggested an
"unfinished" structure, or rather a structure in the process
of completion: two soaring figures whose prolongation in
the air would have formed a gigantic triangle with its apex
reaching for the sky—a powerful, dynamic vision of unity.
For political reasons, this mirror-image, dual bridge solution, was rejected. Only one bridge was approved. This
left a composition with only one inclined pylon. Calatrava
saw in that the possibility of a mutation, rather than the
destruction of his initial idea. Instead of a mirror scheme,
he would build an independent, asymmetrical structure.[1]
In the framework of a poetics of movement, the solitary,
oblique figure of the scheme—as if in the process of construction or, perhaps, destruction—evoked even more
effectively time, transformation, and the birth and death
of structures.

Rather than use back stays, Calatrava allowed the weight
of the concrete-filled steel pylon to counterbalance the deck.
By substituting one set of stay cables with the weight of
the pylon inclined at 58 degrees, he created a new type of
cable-stayed bridge. Spanning 200 meters, thirteen pairs
of stay cables support a hexagonal, steel boxbeam over the
Meandro San Jeronimo River. The spine serves as an
elevated footpath, bisecting cantilevered traffic lanes 1.6
meters below.

17
Alamillo Bridge
Seville, Spain, 1987–92

Facing page
Bridge at night

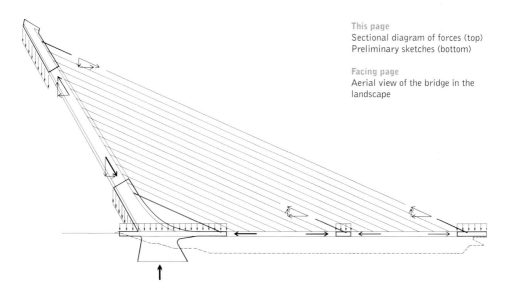

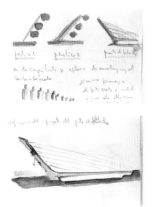

The Alamillo Bridge confounds the assumption that static objects are by nature symmetrical and inherently rigid. Lacking the traditional back stays of most asymmetrical bridges, the Alamillo Bridge incorporates potential energy into the structure: the pylon's mass should tip over backward. Without back stays, the pylon should bend toward the water—pulled by the tension cables and the road deck they are attached to. Calatrava's design achieves structural equilibrium by a sleight-of-hand: the pylon's own weight pulls it downward. The backward cant counteracts the tendency of the roadway stays to bend the tower toward the water. The downward and backward forces on the pylon necessitate a resistance only to vertical forces. This minimizes the mass of the foundation and enables the pylon to gracefully stake its presence in the ground and to direct the pedestrian and automobile movement onto land and beyond.

The bridge undergoes an aesthetic transformation near the 500-meter-long Cartuja Viaduct. Moving through the surrounding landscape, its underside takes the form of a vault, and both of the dual roadways cantilever 5 meters out from the top of the structure, providing shade for pedestrians on the cantilevered promenade decks below. Natural light flows through three continuous rows of circular lightwells, one along the crown of the vault between the two roadways, and the other two at the sides, between the roadway and the promenades.

The meaning of Calatrava's structural innovations and formal inventions is difficult to discern. One must search for clues. In the case of the Alamillo Bridge, the metaphor of the phallus is an obvious yet trite and misleading suggestion. Other images—a harp, a ship's mast, or a swan might also come to mind. Deeper reflection, however, on the structural *raison d'être* of the bridge—carrying horizontal weight—requires a more robust metaphor. The simple image of the human body bearing a weight on its back recasts our perception of the bridge in broader terms. By thinking in terms of a whole body, as opposed to its individual appendages, we can better understand the

Above
Preliminary sketch

Facing page
View from the viaduct

structural relationship between the cables and the horizontal deck, creating a composite image to confound superficial inclinations. The anthropomorphic metaphor makes the engineering feat more familiar; the analogy of the laboring body ennobles both entities.

Both the bridge and the viaduct resist instant categorization by raising questions and by seeking optimal and sculptural answers. Traditional bridges commonly reveal their structural purpose by articulating components of compression, tension, and support. The Alamillo Bridge fuses these elements into a smooth, flowing silhouette. The intersection of tower, bridge deck, and abutment is a sculpted moment that emphasizes the continuity of the bridge without didactically explaining the transfer of loads between components.

The sublime intensity of the pylon reverberates in the landscape on a scale proportionate to that of the river itself, paying homage to the region's environment and its past. The effect is intensified at night, as innovative lighting accentuates the aura of a monument. Rather than hiring outside lighting specialists, Calatrava himself integrated lighting fixtures into a limited number of elements comprising the bridge. Yet the monumentality of the structure is neither stagnant nor nostalgic. The scheme achieves monumentality, as defined by John Ruskin: it unites memory and anticipation. Its "unfinished" state, implied by the leaning pylons and the scheme's asymmetry evoke simultaneously memory (of construction) and anticipation (of destruction). Perhaps even more than the earlier projects, the bridge embodies Calatrava's poetics of movement.

Above
Day view

Facing page
Night view

17: Alamillo Bridge

Below
Site plan

Facing page
Section (top)
Model view showing the bridge in
operation (bottom)

18

Médoc Swingbridge

Bordeaux, France, 1991

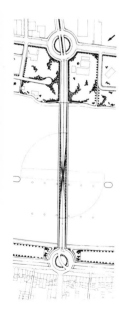

While movement is *implied* by the configuration of the Alamillo Bridge, the design of the Médoc Swingbridge (18), in Bordeaux, France, over the River Garonne, includes actual movement, in the form of a mobile deck that "swings" to let vessels in the river below pass through. Although it was not built, Calatrava's design would have been part of an overall plan for the neighborhood of Port de la Lune. The swingbridge as designed is 240 meters long and sits on a concrete base in the middle of its span. In a seemingly precarious position on the turret is a steel pylon mast stretching 100 meters into the sky.

The bridge's cruciform central section miraculously ties back four sets of fifteen stainless-steel rods, which suspend the road deck below. When the central part of the bridge would rotate, it would reveal two symmetrical gangplanks, extending 88 meters out from the riverbanks. Up to 3 meters above the road deck, the pedestrian decks are entirely separate from the car conduit below. This design decision would enable, among other activities, pedestrians to fish off both sides of each walkway and, below, motorists to have unimpeded views of the water.

The aesthetic impact of the configuration of the Médoc Swingbridge results from the elegance of the structural solution, reminiscent of a graceful ship. The stays define the moving section of the bridge and are reinforced visually by the struts supporting the fixed ends. Without an obvious truss to span the distance, the cables must act as opposite chords in a triangle, closed by a boxbeam, which supports the girders that carry the road deck.

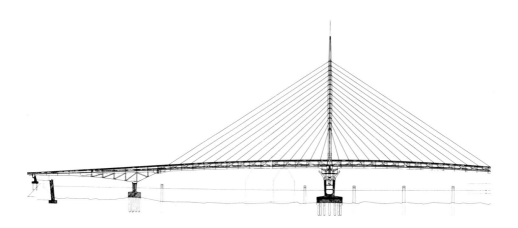

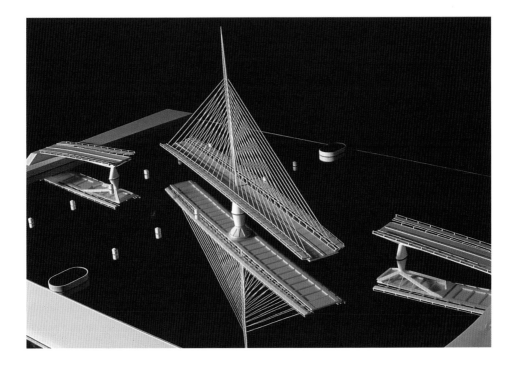

The view from the road is exquisitely designed: a spindle seemingly dances upon the bridge as the stays flatten into minor appendages. In elevation, the pylon seems to be supported by its stays, unlike the other bridges populating the riverscape where pylons clearly support stays. While the slender pylon demonstrates the incredible tensile strength of a stainless-steel cable, it does not make apparent how a thin column can support such weighty material, cars, and people. The graceful shape of the pylon offers clues for understanding its physics: the cruciform profile strengthens the pylon in four directions while simultaneously providing enough area to secure the cable ends. The separation, slant, and single-point meeting of the stays provide counterbalances that require only a pure vertical support. The pylon's thickened midsection provides resistance to buckling, allowing the bottom to taper gracefully.

As with most of Calatrava's ideas, the solution is driven by pragmatic efficiency. The idea behind this clever movement-based solution is to eliminate the need to construct a high bridge deck in order for ships to pass. But in achieving this practical goal, Calatrava's design also achieves a certain poetry: as boats sail past, a person on the bridge would have the fantasy of gracefully plying the current with them. One could see the cable-stayed swingbridge itself, with its 416-meter "mast," transformed into a gliding windjammer, more at home with the boats that go by it than with the cars and pedestrians it carries.

With the Lusitania Bridge (19), the themes of structural and sculptural movement seen in Calatrava's early bridges evolved into sophisticated cultural and environmental

19
Lusitania Bridge
Mérida, Spain, 1988–91

reflections. The bridge was designed in 1988 and built between 1990 and 1991 to span the Guadiana River, which runs through Mérida, Spain. The new bridge runs parallel to a remarkable Roman bridge, which is composed of sixty-four arches and is half a mile long, 10 meters high, and approximately 7 meters wide; it was built under Emperor Augustus two thousand years ago and restored several times. With keen attention to the historical implications of the nearby Roman bridge, Calatrava conceived a 34-meter-deep central steel arch that would support a 189-meter span. The arch dominates the 139-meter side span of

128

This page
View of the bridge and its
reflection (left)
Section showing pedestrian and
vehicle paths (right)

Facing page
Pedestrian path on bridge

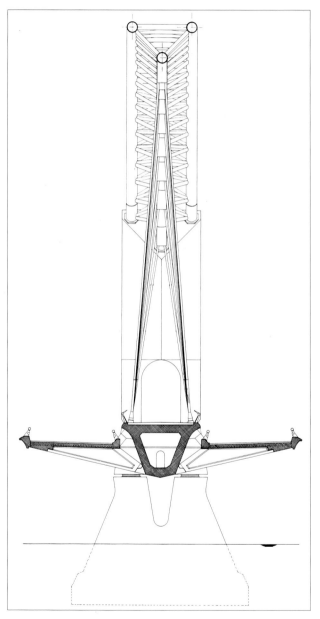

the approaches. Augmenting the arch's presence are a pair of concrete-reinforced springing abutments. These frame the haunch of a tubular-lattice arch-truss, which reflects the mass and material of the ancient Roman bridge, 600 meters upstream. The springing abutments create portals for the bridge's 5.5-meter-wide pedestrian crossing. Similar to the early bridges, the walkway is situated on the top of a boxbeam and is located above the dual roadways to permit unobstructed, panoramic views of the area. This central load-bearing, post-tensioned, and precast concrete torque tube supports prestressed concrete wings, which cantilever the road decks over the river. Within the beam's center span, the steel arch suspends the box girder by way of twenty-three steel rod pairs. Under the approaches, the ancient, rhythmic structure of the Roman bridge dictates the 45-meter spacing of the load-bearing, reinforced-concrete piers. In this way, Calatrava pays further homage to the site and to the tradition of building bridges.

The **Oudry-Mesly Footbridge** (20) further demonstrates Calatrava's ability to exploit the full architectural potential of innovative bridges to benefit users and the local environment. The footbridge links two housing estates separated by a superhighway in the Parisian suburb of Créteil. Completed in September 1988, the design is unique in both its details and its scale. Eight meters tall, the bridge consists of split steel arches supporting a series of crossbeams that carry a 55-meter-long concrete walkway. The horizontal bracing creates a portal framing both entries of the bridge. Suspended cables connect the arches to the exposed ends of the crossbeams with sockets and welded gusset plates, creating an enclosed space below that is

20
Oudry-Mesly Footbridge
Créteil, Paris, France, 1987–88

Facing page
View of the bridge spanning the highway

21
Volantin Footbridge
Bilbao, Spain, 1990–97

enhanced by the structure's distended midsection, tightly spaced stays, and close-knit bracing. Bracing the cross beams laterally are two steel I-beams whose curve mirrors the arches above. They terminate where steel fillets at each end of the arch structure transfer the bridge loads into the reinforced-concrete foundations. This fine detailing enhances the human focus of the bridge, providing sharp contrast to the car-filled no man's land below it.

In 1994, in the Spanish town of Bilbao, Calatrava worked once again on a human scale to redesign the Volantin Footbridge (21), which now stands as a unique presence within the town's urban landscape. An inclined, 14.6-meter-deep arch consisting of a pipe 4.57-centimeters in diameter, opposes the 75-meter-wide curbed boardwalk it supports. The sweeping parabolic form of the arch rests delicately, almost impossibly, on the extended armatures of the 2-meter-wide access ramp's triangular-shaped supports. Accentuating the visual illusions is the translucent deck.

Floating 8.5 meters over Bilbao's Nervión River with a width between 6.5 and 7.5 meters, the board's flooring consists of glass plates. A galvanized steel grid, composed of forty-one I-shaped steel ribs with variable sections, runs along the outside of the glass flooring and supports the stainless-steel profiles. As with the Alamillo Bridge, lighting plays a critical role. The light sources were specially designed by Calatrava and are located between the steel ribs, illuminating the floor from underneath; additional lighting is placed in the handrails, stairs, and ramps. Its nighttime brilliance turns the bridge into light sculpture—a beacon to bring together the community.

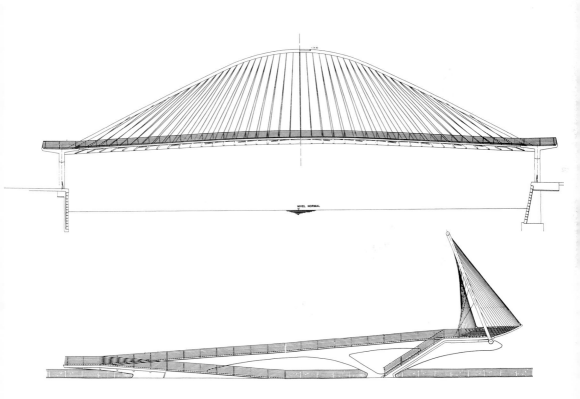

Above
Elevations

Facing page
View from the riverside

21: Volantin Footbridge

Above
Views of the bridge in the day
(left) and at night (right)

Facing page
View under the bridge

As Calatrava's bridges became more adventurous structurally, they began to more eloquently define the identity of the place in which they were situated. The uniqueness of the structures brings into relief the singularity of the landscape that contains them, as if giving back to the environment what they subtracted through the space they occupy. One of the most remarkable of these structures is the **La Devesa Footbridge** (22), in the town of Ripoll, north of Barcelona in the Pyrenees. Designed in 1989, it spans 44 meters over the Ter River to connect the town center with the railway station. To accommodate a grade change of 5 meters over a 65-meter span, Calatrava used a canted steel arch to carry the loads of a timber walkway from an existing retaining wall across to a new concrete pylon.

Although the original design was altered by a local engineer hired by municipal authorities to design a corbel at one end of the bridge, Calatrava's concept and overall design remain intact. This is seen most clearly in the elegance of the structural systems. Steel tension arms, lying within the plane of the 6.5-meter-deep arch, take the walkway loads. As these loads deflect both the walkway and the tension arms, the angle of the arch changes, moving to a vertical position. The natural rotation of the elliptical deck moves the tension arms into position to brace the plane of the arch and stiffen it against buckling. The tubular steel spine of the bridge collects torsion at each strut, delivering it to the pylon and the retaining wall. Below, a cross-truss directly beneath the walkway prevents lateral distortion, completing a holistic system of structure, architecture, and context. The physical feats accomplished by this structure seem appropriate for the

22

La Devesa Footbridge

Ripoll, Spain, 1989–91

Above
Model

Facing page
The bridge in the landscape

timeless, rugged landscape of the Pyrenees. At the same time, the bridge offers to the people of the surrounding area a renewed sense of place and purpose.

An equally outstanding contribution to the landscape and to the local community is the **Puerto Bridge** (23). The structural and functional statements are minimal: a delicately balanced single arch spanning 71 meters over the port of Ondarroa, Spain, at the mouth of the Artibay River. The deck separates yet synthesizes two 4.5-meter-wide pedestrian walkways with a central 7-meter-wide vehicular crossing. The 15-meter-deep asymmetric steel arch carries both the box-girder vehicular deck and the curved, cantilevered pedestrian deck. While the arch takes vertical loads from stay-cables, it is braced against buckling by inclined tension arms loaded by the sheer weight of the seaside pedestrian walkway. Although the three passageways have a constant width, the seaside walkway bows outward to trace a semicircle; as the deck increases in height, the cantilever increases, too, as it nears the midpoint of the bridge. This banked surface creates an important space between itself and the rest of the bridge floor. Structurally, the extension is critical: it counterbalances the opposite side of the bridge precisely where more support is needed—at the midpoint.

Seen from some distance above, the circular elements of the bridge echo the curves of the harbor and town. Seen from below, they reflect the gentle curves of the surrounding hills. As with Ronchamp, one becomes more aware of the character and the uniqueness of the landscape thanks to the presence of the sculpture-structure of the bridge.

23
Puerto Bridge
Ondarroa, Spain, 1989–95

Facing page
The bridge in its urban and landscape context

Above
The bridge and the harbor

Facing page
The bridge and the pedestrian
path to its left

While the Puerto Bridge keeps a relatively quiet profile and clings to the landscape, the **Alameda Bridge and Underground Station** (24), in Valencia, Spain, seems strangely incomplete, giving the illusion of instability. In a way, the design reflects the environmental precariousness of the site, an abandoned space created by the redirection of the Turia River, which left an interrupted, unresolved relation between two sides of an urban community. Built between 1991 and 1995, the bridge is composed of 130 meters of road deck and cantilevered pedestrian walkway, which connect the historical center of Valencia to the university quarter. Past and future lie on opposite sides of a parched Turia riverbed and a vibrant subterranean metro station.

The once distinct domains of the horizontal and the vertical dizzyingly merge in the form of a 70-degree leaning arch. Rising 14 meters above the deck, the arch's cant seems illusory—an arch can only be upright. Compounding the confusion are the regularly spaced steel suspension rods, which insure the planar stability of the arch. Their frequency and size would imply a sibling arch, which is notably absent. The weight of the tilted arch and pedestrian deck offset the weight of the road deck and car loads, eliminating the need for a secondary arch. A thickened moment joint distributes these loads to chords lying in the plane of the canted arch. The arch itself maintains a constant cross-section by combining two steel tubes of different diameter and enclosing them in sheet metal to form a triangular section. Expanding upon the structural principles of an I-beam, a smaller tube projects outward from a larger steel tube to improve its resistance to

24
Alameda Bridge and Underground Station
Valencia, Spain, 1991–95

Facing page
Pedestrian and vehicle paths

buckling. Structural optimization enables the arch to carry the loads to the far ends of the banks of the riverbed and deliver these forces into the ground.

This structural balancing act is possible only if the arch itself is prevented from buckling. To this end, Calatrava ingeniously deployed a well-known feature of suspension structures to turn the bridge into an integrated structural system. Cables generally increase stability by the constant tension of the weight they support. This interdependence, in turn, improves the strength of the individual elements. Calatrava achieved a similar result: by constructing the bridge deck in four boxed sections, he ensured that the bridge works as an arch-structure rather than as a curved beam. The deck dramatically improves the rigidity of the arch by preventing it from moving out of its plane. As gravity loads deflect both the road deck and tension arms, the arms themselves rotate the arch slightly into a more upright position, which stiffens the members to resist buckling.

The bridge gives the impression of a singular element, neither dominating the surrounding landscape nor frivolous, yet rich in connotations. The tiled arch defines a distinct place and encourages views away from the void and the traffic. As the arch emerges from the deck, it not only expresses its structural virtue by holding up the entire bridge, but it also performs the figurative gesture of marking the location of the metro station below ground. The station itself maintains a link to the surface by means of a nonslip, ribbed roof of translucent glass that defines a plaza at ground level.

Facing page
The bridge in its urban context

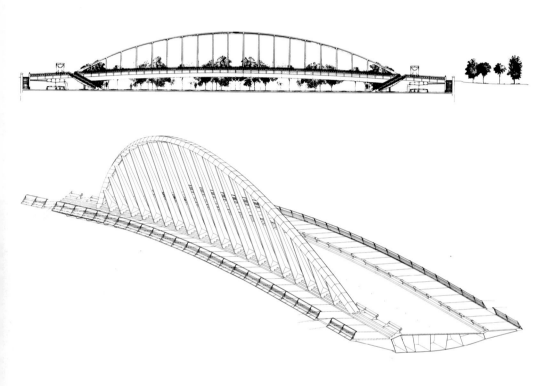

Above
Side elevation (top)
Axonometric drawing (bottom)

Facing page
Entry to the underground station

The station itself is divided into three levels: the entry level consists of the translucent, paved plaza with openings to the ticketing level below. From the ticketing level, located at either end of the station, one can see the full length and double-height space of the platform below, and the ribbed, translucent roof structure above. Enclosing the space are double-wall concrete and brick side retaining walls. Molded into the top of these retaining walls are skylights, which bring both light and ventilation into the station and, at night, define the edges of the entry-level plaza outside. The actual movement—of trains and

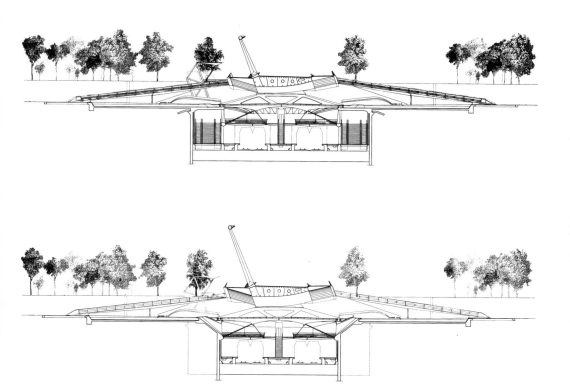

Above
Side elevation (top)
Section (bottom)

Facing page
View of the underground station

25

Tenerife Exhibition Hall

Tenerife, Spain, 1992–95

passengers—that the station contains, and the potential movement incorporated in the configuration of the structure, invigorate an otherwise dispirited site caught between abandonment and unfulfilled potential. The structures also reestablish the flow between two previously disjointed urban communities.

In the bridges we have discussed up to now, the poetics of movement applied to mobile parts or parts that channeled vehicles and transported people. It also applied to configurations, to parts of the structure whose abstract geometry tacitly suggested process and change. Calatrava's analogies to living organisms are made on the basis of systems and functions, rather than on appearance.

An exception to these substantive metaphors is the architect's design for the **Tenerife Exhibition Hall** (25), located in the Spanish Canary Islands and designed to resemble a bird. The building's various parts recall rib, wing, and beak, creating an overall effect of a gigantic creature of flight resting by the sea. One can make up stories, seeing it as a sea-bird ready to take off for distant journeys. The aesthetic effect is strong because of the affinity of the image with the landscape and because of Calatrava's careful attention to detail.

The building uses one structural spanning element as *the* motif to cover the entire complex, which occupies a site of 48,500 square meters. Calatrava constructed a single steel arch with concrete buttresses to span 270 meters over the complex. Hanging from this structural spine is a shallower, secondary arch, supporting a symmetric series

of triangulated trusses (using the Jakem truss motif),
which touch down onto 18-meter-high A-frames set within
the exterior curtain wall. The resulting 142-by-68-meter
rectangular space creates a multipurpose, support-free hall
flexible enough to accommodate minor private and major
public events, including large trade fairs and the annual
Tenerife Carnival. The deck of the interior hall is built
into the landscape on one side and supported by a glazed
and buttressed plinth facing north toward the park and the
sea beyond.

Above
Interior view

Facing page
Interior view

26
Lyons Airport Railway Station
Satolas, Lyons, France, 1989–94

Similar mimetic strategies are employed in the design of the Lyons Airport Railway Station (26). Here, however, we see icons used in skillful combination with more abstract design strategies, implying movement through geometry, as with the bridge projects already examined. Like a bridge, the Lyons Airport Railway Station can be seen as an elongated, complex amalgam of structure, conduit, and spanning constructs. The station is the terminus for high-speed trains connecting the airport to Lyons, 30 kilometers to the south. It also materializes the clients' vision for a functional yet exciting symbolic structure, and represents the first realization of Calatrava's extensive three-dimensional experiments in spanning, enclosure, and movement. Unlike the site for the Stadelhofen Railway Station, with its tight topographical, historical, and man-made constraints, the site of the Lyons Station did not restrict the form of the structure. Basically, the scheme comprises a main station building, with train platforms, and a passageway connecting the station to the adjacent airport it serves. The program called for a design that provided directional orientation—an important utilitarian, as well as psychological, objective when serving hurried travelers. This requirement presented a fresh challenge to Calatrava.

Rather than orienting the movement of travelers using signs within an undistinguished enclosure, or a "universal space," as many designers of contemporary terminals have chosen to do, Calatrava channels and informs crowds through the configuration of the building itself. This explains the size and the strong sense of direction given to the elements of the complex and justifies the rhythmic

Facing page
Exterior view

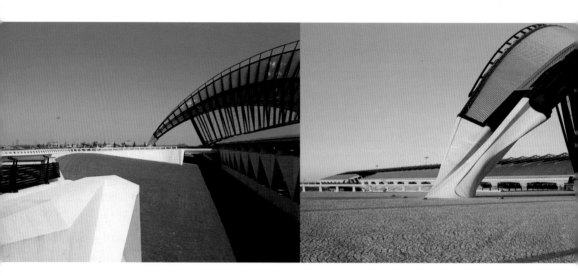

repetition of structural members as they relate to the movement of the crowds. The need for orientation also explains the modulation of light, also conceived in a directional and rhythmic way. Light is more sparse in the core of the station, becoming more abundant toward the tracks and the outside. Through these design strategies Calatrava endeavors to transform contemporary travel from a drudgery into a memorable, even romantic experience.

Entering from the upper deck, a concrete V-shaped abutment joins the ends of four steel arches as they lunge forward to greet the visitor. The center pair of arches follows

Above
Four views of the structural bracing of the main hall at the front (this page) and back (facing page)

the line of the roof to form a spine composed of baffled vertebrae. The outer aluminum-clad surface chambers reach a height of 40 meters. The adjacent pair of curved beams spans 120 meters over an expansive, glazed station hall and eastern service core, which contains ticket offices, retail shops, and other amenities. The vertebrae spread like wings over the north and south facades, whose bulging mullions support the cantilevered span. Embodying circulation and travel, these projected, curved sheaths seemingly glide upward on the warm air currents from the trains racing below. Surrounding the tracks and train platforms are 53 meters of continuous support and

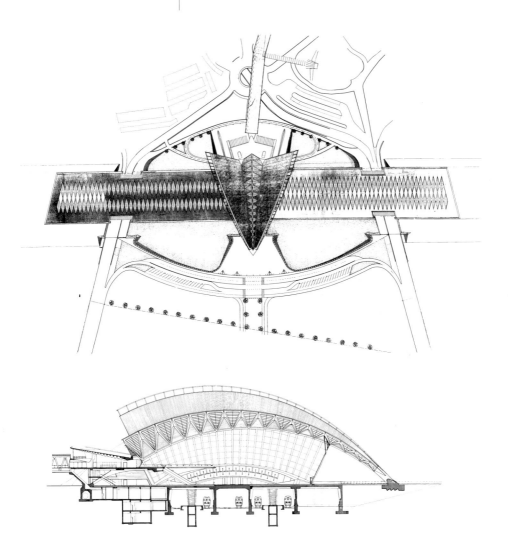

Interpenetration of channels
and structure

coverage. Cast on site and resembling a hive, inverted concrete elements rhythmically support the platform roof and
visually complement the roof modules in the main termi-
nal area. Above the tracks, concrete vaults of intersecting,
diagonal arches span the platform. The weblike laminated
roof is open to the sky; above the platforms, it is either
glazed or filled with prefabricated concrete sections. Such
rhythmic elements give visitors cues to the overall design
and subtly guide them in their movement through the
station.

Bridges are a complex combination of construction and
conduit intended to overcome yawning fissures or deep
clefts in the earth's surface, such as rivers, ravines, and
man-made obstructions like highways. Calatrava's highly
synthetic design approach—his impulse to connect very
disparate elements—is in itself an act of "bridging" and is
naturally suited to the real-world task of bridge-building.
Perhaps it is through the bridge, more than any other type
of structure Calatrava designs, that he succeeds in fusing
engineering and sculpture, science and art. Through his
bridges he has demonstrated how design can unite the
environment and act as a catalyst to enhance the landscape, improve the quality of urban life, and restore
communication and community.

Chapter Five
Infrastructure and Dream-work Projects

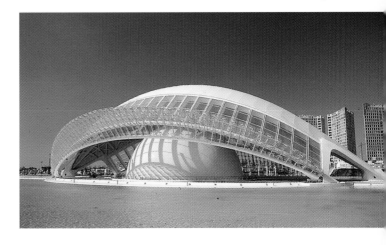

Calatrava's explosive career throughout the 1990s is marked by a number of very large-scale projects in terms of size, context, and complexity. Characteristic of the development of these projects is the continuous reuse and recombination of themes and types conceived in the first five years of his career. Structural motifs, spatial themes, and stories, familiar from earlier work, reappear essentially reinterpreted. Calatrava has rethought these precedents as he has become increasingly involved with the study of the unique character of a site. This engagement with existing conditions and the constraints of the surrounding context highlights both the site's hidden adversities and its latent potentials. In confronting the meanness of the environment, not uncommon in many of the urban projects, one also discovers and embraces its richness.

As Calatrava's design solutions become more complex and the sophistication of their technology advances, the wildest metaphors become more persistent. Dream-work becomes manifest, as in the awakening-eye image of the **Planetarium of the Valencia Science Center** (27), in Camino de las Moreras in Valencia, Spain, Calatrava's hometown. In 1991 Calatrava won the competition to develop a complex for a science museum and planetarium on the southern banks of the dried-up bed of the Turia River, not far from the bridge he would complete in 1995. Once more, Calatrava was faced with a challenging task: to design within the context of a peripheral, abandoned, and, at the time, hopeless area.

Within the complex, Calatrava conceived a scheme of a transparent, concrete arched pod, 110 meters long and 55.5 meters wide, to house a globe-shaped planetarium. The form and operation of the structure is seductive and tantalizing: at the side of the pod an enormous movable door opens and closes, revealing the spherical planetarium, as the eyelid covers and uncovers the eye. The eye association becomes even more striking as the graceful, hypnotic movements of the structure are mirrored in shallow reflecting pools—reminders of the site's fluvial past—surrounding the complex.

The "lid" incorporates a system of slats mounted on pivoting central stems. As the mobile structures slowly open out, they reveal the interior of the sphere, simultaneously giving it a light and floating appearance and strengthening the dream atmosphere rather than the naturalistic imitation. Once the sphere is revealed, the image of a globe emerges, invoking its symbolic identification with the universe. The eye, the primary point of entry for knowledge, then becomes both receptor and that which is perceived—at once subject and object.

27
Planetarium of the Valencia Science Center
Valencia, Spain, 1991

Facing page
Detail view of the planetarium
and concrete arched pod

Above
Planetarium and reflecting pool

Facing page
Complex at night, showing the
canopy in opened and half-closed
positions

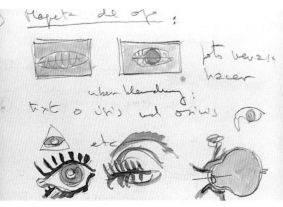

Above
Preliminary sketch (left)
Three views of the concrete and
glass canopy in operation (right)

Facing page
Section (bottom)

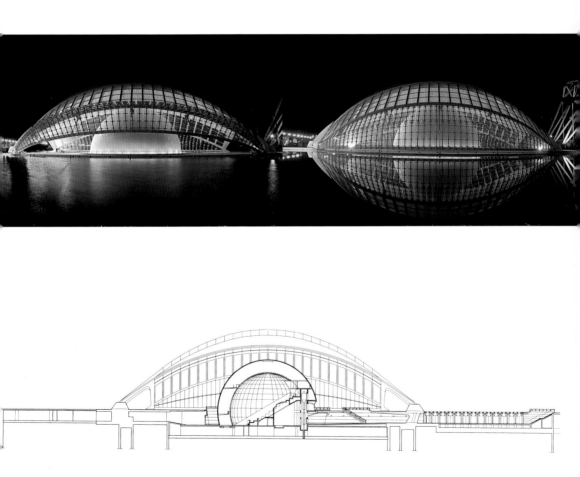

28

Cathedral of St. John the Divine

New York, New York, 1991

Like Antonio Gaudí's unfinished Catalan masterpiece, the Sagrada Famila, Calatrava's prize-winning 1991 design to complete the **Cathedral of St. John the Divine** (28) in New York converts secular stone, steel, and glass into the disciplinary deities of place, engineering, and aesthetics. The project revitalizes traditional architectural form by reinterpreting its structure. St. John the Divine is an Episcopalian cathedral, on which construction was begun in 1892. Originally designed in the style of its Gothic predecessors, it is, though still unfinished today, the world's largest cathedral. The church's tripartite elevation dominates both the existing spatial composition and the newly proposed configuration. Apexes of the existing facade vertically inform the low nave roof—a glass- and steel-covered green garden walkway offering visitors views of New York City. The new structure accentuates and integrates the existing southern entry, while the northern entry becomes a synthesis of architecture and engineering, indicating the idea of an entry. Inside, the long, narrow, and high transversal space muses on the great cathedrals of the past, while pediments evoke the ribbed sections of Gothic-age masterworks.

Calatrava continues to follow a traditional construction pattern by using the lower spaces paralleling the nave and transept to support the higher, central spaces. At the chancel, architectural contours gradually lift the eyes toward a spire and to heaven beyond. In a sort of "Garden of Eden," 50 meters above the intersection of the crucifix plan, lies the cathedral's crowning feature—a biosphere. First proposed by Buckminster Fuller, the biosphere was presented to church officials as an opportunity to bring ecology into

Facing page
Model view of southern transept
showing original cathedral and
proposed intervention

a place of worship. Calatrava's realization is a large, circular open space that allows visitors to the bioshelter to look down into the expansive cathedral and above to the heavenly spire. By replacing the original timber construction with lightweight materials and introducing a system of rotating panels, Calatrava's design creates a structure that allows light, air, and rain into the celestial garden when the panels are opened. The result is a natural climate control for the cathedral: warm, fresh air generated in the roof space is drawn downward into the nave and crypt. Without doubt, however, there are poetic and symbolic implications in the scheme.

Calatrava's homily on form and the forces it wrestles with is an invitation to seek new architectural understanding. By re-representing the typology of Gothic construction, Calatrava shows us precedent in a new light, educating newcomers about architecture, structure, and the aesthetics of built form. It is more than a mere love affair with tradition; Calatrava uses precedent, in the form of the given physical fabric of the building as well as its meaning, inherited from history, to enable innovation. The reborn cathedral poses a religious polemic—respect through interpretation, learning from the past to deal with the present and seek the future.

Once more the tension between memory and invention, recollection and anticipation, tradition and permanence, observance and search are parameters that define the poetics of movement, this time in an even more metaphorical manner. Unfortunately, there are no current plans to build Calatrava's design.

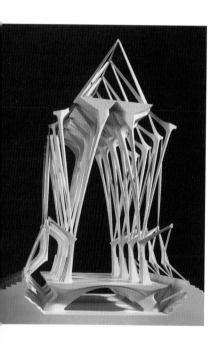

Above
Model of the nave structure

Facing page
Sections (left)
Plan of garden level (right)

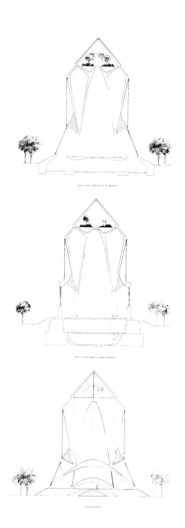

29
Reichstag
Berlin, Germany, 1992

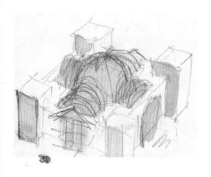

Since architecture deeply affects human relations, it is unavoidably political, at least in part. Form emerges from human negotiation, and inhabitants redefine meaning and use daily. Walls witness mankind's struggles and mark historical events. Buildings are intended as referent in a public, civic discourse. They exude significance, represent power, and legitimate order. The forces imbuing architecture with a profundity beyond function permeate the original German parliament building in Berlin, the Reichstag (29), and Calatrava's 1992 proposal for its refurbishment. Built by militaristic Prussians in 1894 to unify a fragmented German nation, it was damaged both in 1933, by Nazi arson, and again during World War II. Until 1991, when the newly reunified German government chose to return to Berlin, the building had been a constant reminder of German aggression. Impregnated with a turbulent history and, now, with a spirit of reconciliation, the new Reichstag merges people, events, and symbol to set forth an architectural challenge of unprecedented civic relevance. Accordingly, the international competition to renovate the building proved equally turbulent. Calatrava's entry, though not ultimately selected, was taken over and used in the winning scheme—a fact that raised many provocative questions.

Calatrava responded to the challenge by addressing the building's political character. His controversial decision to revisit the unrealized dome of the original architect constituted a daring confrontation with the past, and a critical vision for the future. Beyond the obvious material differences, vis-à-vis the original dome, the undulating roof form proposed by Calatrava heightens orthogonal rigidity,

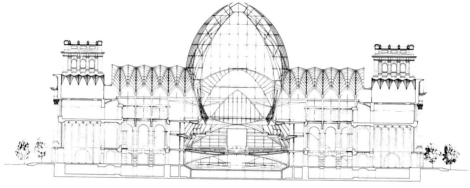

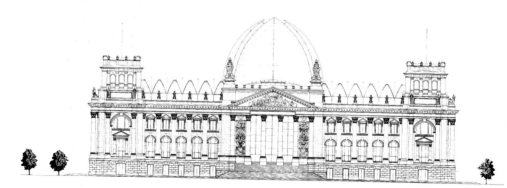

Above
Section (top)
Elevation (bottom)

Facing page
Model view of glass dome in
operation

Below
Elevation sketch study (top)
Preliminary sketch showing
domed auditorium (bottom)

Facing page
Photomontage

positing a deliberate contrast between the revivalist style
and a contemporary idiom. Its proportional relationship to
the symmetrical classicist facade and the nearby Branden-
burg Gate preserves the status of the original building. The
glass dome crowns the junction of the four extruded cor-
nices, and the new roof structure takes its rhythm from
the existing proportions. Within, triangulated steel trusses
resting on the original masonry walls span two vaulted,
enclosed courtyards. Above, a filigree structural system
mobilizes Calatravian motifs and implies potential
movement.

If the dome emerges from the dichotomies of past and
future, it also represents the tensions of a moment in
history full of potential for change. The glass dome transgresses the sacrosanct height of the original facade, and yet
it is contained by it. The dome's undulating roof reflects
the turbulence of politics below the roof's pristine veneer.
The ultimate polemic is manifest in the potential movement of the dome: Calatrava hinted of the demand for
metamorphosis and transformation by articulating the
edges of the four large, petal-shaped segments. Pivoting
on the public gallery's inner edge, above the assembly,
each petal opens upward from a central closed point. By
ingeniously using the tensile strength of cables to brace the
structure and carry the glazed exterior skin, Calatrava minimized structural dimensions to bestow movement on the
dome. Additionally, manipulation of the hall's lighting enables
the historical landmark to glow dramatically in darkness.

By architecturally rejuvenating the paradoxes and potentials of a historically charged monument, Calatrava posed

an implicit challenge: How will the tensions be resolved? He himself avoids the stasis of the past and the seduction of the future through the movement inherent to the present. The interior structure leaps from a public forum below the assembly to integrate heterogeneous elements into a new mosaic of diversity and wonder. The intricate roof system reflects the complexity of the city and the potential to create coherence out of the ashes of the past. It evokes the fact that political rebirth contains the potential for a rich culture to blossom once more. The symbolic importance of the dome and its movement can be seen as reaching beyond technical and historical interpretations; it projects a dialogue of politics, history, and people into the future. It endows the building with a literal and figurative crown— a guiding metaphor for the moral responsibilities to come.

30

Alcoy Community Hall

Alcoy, Spain, 1992–95

Whereas Calatrava used the Reichstag project to explore architecture's morality, he was more concerned with architecture's everyday dimension in designing the **Alcoy Community Hall** (30), in Spain in 1995. The hall is situated in the heart of the town's Plaza España, site of the festival of St. George and other community events. To preserve the historical nature of the site, Calatrava created a subterranean multiuse civic hall with a capacity of six hundred— idea for civil weddings and general exhibitions. Translucent glass floor panels attached to stainless-steel frames let light into the hall by day and emit a diffuse, mild glow by night that illuminates the plaza above. Above ground, a fountain, lights, and an enclosed entrance break the continuity of the plaza surface to announce the presence of the underground space. Both the fountain and the entrance employ moving rod-and-joint mechanisms that produce the effect of a veil or drape—a variation on the doors of the Ernsting Warehouse and on the "eyelid" of the planetarium in Valencia. Building on the previous cases, the movement produced here is surprising, strange, and, in this fountain, even eerie. As with the doors of the Ernsting Warehouse, Calatrava draws on both the technological principles of his Ph.D. dissertation and on the motor-spatial investigations of his sculptural experiments. The hypnotic movement of the stainless-steel door, which reveals an entrance cavity and stairs, as well as the folding cover of the spring-fed circular pool, at the opposite end of the plaza, offer a provocative prelude to the puzzles and marvels under the pavement of the plaza.

A 9-meter descent leads into an 80-meter-long hall enveloped by a riblike reinforced-concrete structure with a

stucco and plaster finish. Rising 6 meters high and spanning the 18-meter width of the hall, the ribs support the roof and extend from a large arch, built along the longitudinal axis, to which is affixed a series of evenly spaced single-cast radiating arches. The combination of the opaque, horizontal surfaces atop the arches and the glass panels fitted between them create the alternating rhythm of the roof. The intersection of the pairs of symmetrical arches creates a correspondingly marked valley along the longitudinal axis, which in turn cradles a longitudinal supporting arch springing from the east end. The configuration of the arches employs typical Calatravian structural themes, yet there is something very traditional about the way the elements relate to each other to instill a sense of movement.

Like Jonah, we pass through an esophagus to find ourselves within the whale, where a longitudinal sternum

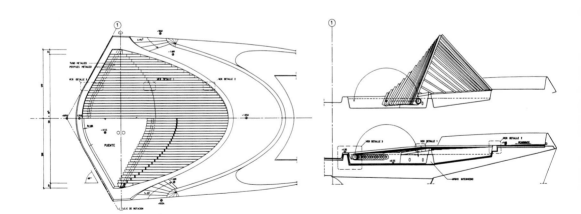

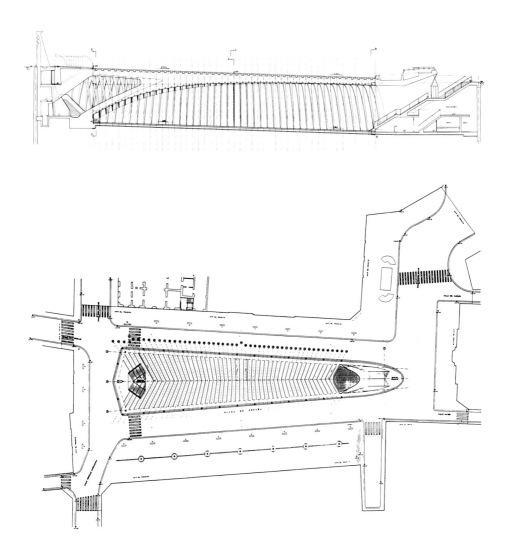

Above
Section (top)
Plan (bottom)

Facing page
Main hall

supports the repetitive arches of a rib cage. However, upon closer observation, anomalies confound this organic metaphor to reveal an unfamiliar sinew of structure and sculpture. The arches do not support the ceiling; their ends come gracefully to a point, and they are occasionally suspended in mid-air rather than resting on the ground in broad support. The ribs do not shape external form; they are held back from vertical walls. As the form of the single arch changes to a dual arch, a new, intricate, and intervening form is introduced between the two as a transitional element. The cavity's complex organization transcends dogmas of formal purity. This is unequivocally an enigmatic structure and, even more so, an ambiguous spatial configuration. The proximate cohabitation of the arch and rib themes appears to be an anomaly—but a welcome one—for spatial and structural anomalies invite interrogation and fuel the search for answers and learning.

Above
Main entry descending to the hall

Facing page
Secondary stair to the hall

31

Orient Station

Lisbon, Portugal, 1993–98

For the **Orient Station** (31), Calatrava went beyond the original scope of the competition brief to create a veritable oasis, a zone of urban fertility in the middle of a once run-down industrial wasteland on the coast just north of Lisbon, Portugal. Taking on a project that was originally intended merely as a transport connection for the 1998 World's Fair, Calatrava sought to move the Orient Station into the realm of urban planning. He cultivated the remnants of a derelict harbor to create a nexus of high-speed intercity trains, standard rail services, regional bus lines, underground parking lots, and subterranean metro links. By locating the station on existing railway lines, he transformed an embankment that had historically separated residences from industry into a civic link. He started by raising the station platform 11 meters off the ground onto a bridge structure. This allows the existing perpendicular avenue to run seamlessly into the complex. The avenue's continuation 152 meters beyond the station visually reinforces the ease of movement between all the various transport modes.

As with the Zurich and Lyons transportation projects, the mutual relationship between site and program weaves together the romance of distant travels, the satisfaction of hard work, and the spirit of dream-work. The complexity of Calatrava's solution brings many analogies to mind. The platform/oasis, "forested" with "tree" columns, is also a Mediterranean-style open market. A scalloped awning of glass and steel welcomes travelers to new experiences. Gentle concrete arches speak of wind-worn artifacts, smoothed to perfection by nature's forces. They cascade over a multilevel reef of boutiques, ticket counters, and

Facing page
View of the rail platform/oasis

Above
The station in its urban context

Facing page
Overall view of the railway station
and bus station

platform access areas. Beyond this sanctuary, a glass-and-steel canopy, cresting 5 meters high to cover 11-meter-wide bus platforms, alludes in its shape to the waves of the nearby sea. Fourteen meters above, palms of steel and glass flourish on a 17-meter grid. In a tree-structure motif, parasols merge column and roof, and branches intertwine to cover eight railway lines.

Above
Glass and steel canopies over
train platforms

Above
Night view of bus lanes with elevated train platforms in distance

Facing page
Circulation between train platforms and ground transportation

If the Orient Station is a loosely covered enclosure that unites tree themes and conduits, the Milwaukee Art Museum (32) is an all-encompassing, all-enveloping cover. The forestlike scheme of the Orient Station roofs suggests the virtual movement of branches, invoking escape. By contrast, the museum's uniquely mobile roof structure notably accommodates functional changes but also, through its avian grace—a theme also used in the Church of Year 2000 competition entry—suggests the specificity and significance of the location.

Begun in 1994, the complex expands upon an existing site composed of Eero Saarinen's 1957 War Memorial and a squat structure built in 1975. Calatrava's design bestows upon the site a reinvigorated architectural identity and functional clarity. By complementing and enhancing the existing buildings and site, Calatrava creates an ensemble— an interplay of built structure and gardens with waterfront views. He complements Saarinen's original structure, an 11-meter-high arched, laminated roof of glazed and stainless steel, that stretches 134 meters along Lake Michigan's shore. Taking additional geometric cues from the existing buildings and the shoreline, the 7,500 square meters of additional museum space consistently seek out the lake, while the roof tapers to 6 meters to maintain the existing vistas.

Movement from the existing structure to the new one is directed perpendicularly by an extended footbridge that invites pedestrians from the city to leave urbanity behind in a flight of fancy. The cable-stay bridge builds on the traditional vertical pylon plan to extend the span to 73

32

Milwaukee Art Museum
Milwaukee, Wisconsin, 1994–2000

Facing page
Site context with existing museum building, gardens, and lakeshore

meters. Its 50-meter-high spine stands at a 47-degree
incline and provides a partial counterbalance to the bridge
deck. A geometric arrangement of the return anchorage
cables enables the mast to carry the entire load and accentuates the kinetic transition from street-bound movement
to soaring flight. The inclined mast provides a directional
prelude to the focal point of the entire composition.

The unfurling roof, lying at the intersection of the laminated gallery and webbed tensile footbridge, moves the
observer beyond the complex and surrounding environment. The conical form lies at rest as a volume extruded
upward from the gallery, while carrying on its back the
implicit movement of the bridge. Functionally designed as

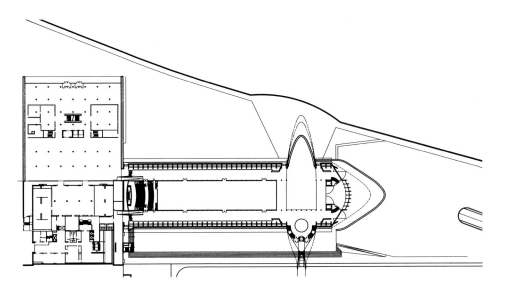

Above
Four views of roof study models in motion

Facing page
Model views with the roof system in opened and closed positions

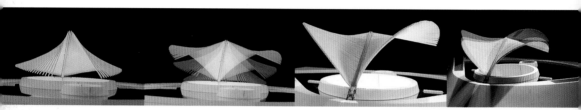

entry and temporary exhibition space, the pavilion transcends the geometry, materials, and volumes of the existing buildings to redefine the museum's identity. In a striking pose, the louvered surface rises 60 meters to create shade and a sense of wonder, combining once again structure and sculpture. The structure hovers majestically alongside the shore of the lake, signaling entry and event. Certainly the mobile roof structure serves functional mobility, but, like so many of Calatrava's projects, it also serves as a graceful, even playful, nondidactic representation of the cognitive challenges his design embodies.

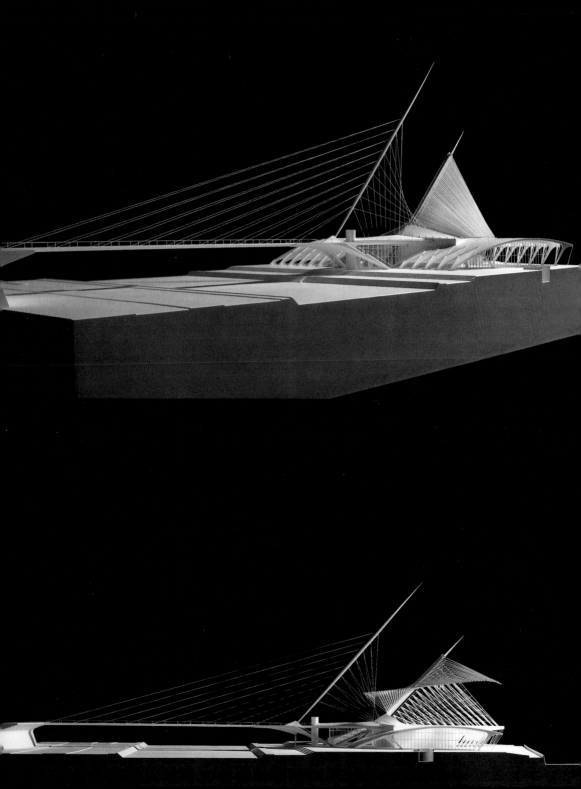

Chapter Six
Poetry in Motion

Buildings, engineering works, sculptures, and furniture by Santiago Calatrava demonstrate the genius of one of the greatest, most prolific designers of our time, and, furthermore, reveal him to be one of the very few designers in any field who can be called a universal designer. Within a short period of time, he has succeeded in producing a vast number of diverse projects and forging a new approach to design that fuses structure and movement, a poetics of morphology. Calatrava transcends distinctions between architecture, technology, and art, and in the process transforms buildings and infrastructure from mere utilitarian objects to land art and public sculpture. He regards the divisions between tradition and innovation, creation and reflection as social establishments and institutional demarcations rather than as natural distinctions. He synthesizes problem-solving and dream-work into an iconoclastic cultural vision by exploiting the ubiquitous act of movement.

Applying problem-solving methods to design, Calatrava shapes optimal schemes that minimize resources and maximize performance. As we have seen, he systematically employs *profiling*: he shapes variably the contour of structural members, and he locates material ideally to counteract changing forces that can cause structural failure. Profiling results in the swollen midsections or corners and the tapered ends so typical of Calatrava's structural elements. Equally methodical, as we have seen, is his application of *differentiation*: he separates structural members according to their function and specializes their material to best suit their assigned performance.

Below
Sculpture study with cube

Facing page
Sketches for sculptures with the
Alamillo Bridge (17)

33

Drawings and Sculptures

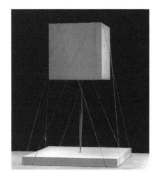

Profiling and differentiation, it should be understood, are applied only after Calatrava has conceived the configuration of the scheme—the overall composition of the structure or the arrangement and articulation of the components. It is in this very early but decisive conceptual phase in the design process—a phase surrounded by an aura of mystery—that major breakthroughs, but also many serious errors, can occur. Calatrava excels in this highly creative phase. It is here that we see most clearly the universality of his thinking and his capacity to synthesize.

There are two highly polarized ways to invent a design scheme: the analytical and the analogical. In the context of the division of labor and the institutional split of Western architecture and design, engineers prefer the first, and architects and artists the second. Calatrava employs both.

In his theoretical study "On the Foldability of Space Frames," completed at the Swiss Federal Institute of Technology (ETH), Calatrava took the analytical path. We have already seen how he developed a general method to transform all possible types of space frames into planar shapes and lines, similar to the way an umbrella opens as a broad plane or folds into a stick. As a result of his research, Calatrava found in the method a very useful tool that enabled him to make structures spread easily in all directions, taking different forms. He could give concrete form to his visions of fluid, waving structures, and incorporate them into any component of a project that could move with and adapt to a world in flux. These visions can perhaps be traced to the wonder he felt as a child at Le Corbusier's

1

2

3

4

12

16

11

5

6

7

8

10

9

13

14

ver hialete 10
figuras o 12
figuras

This page and facing page
Sculpture studies with cubes

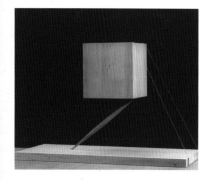

chapel at Ronchamp and to some of the aspirations of his
generation of May 1968.

It is obvious that designers rely on analysis only to a very
limited degree. In most cases "creative" design is motivated by imagination, intuition, or insight. These terms,
however, indicating the act of looking "inside," disclose
very little about the complexity of thinking that generates
original designs or about the nature of the "mysterious"

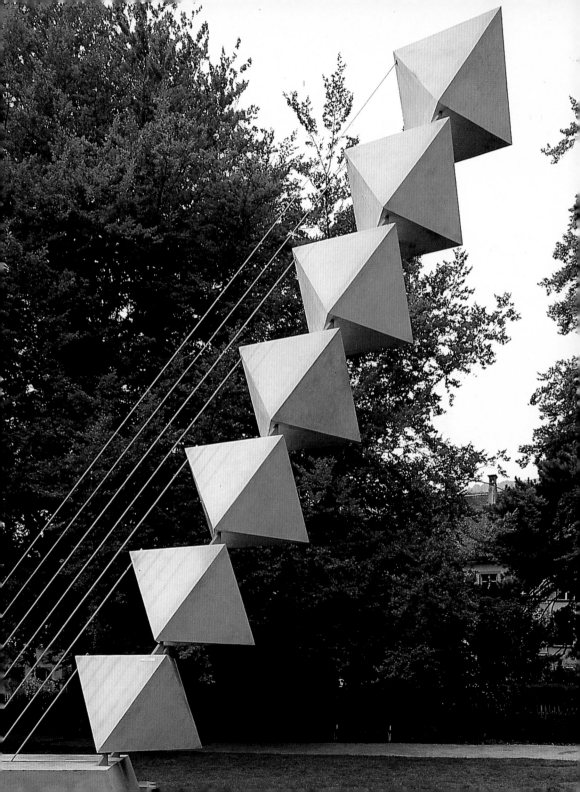

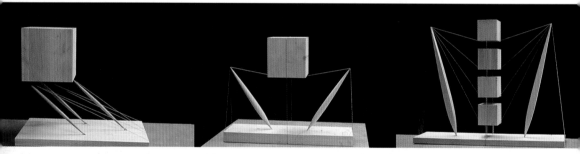

Above
Sculpture studies with cubes

Facing page
Twisted spine sculpture

mind that gives birth to what Herbert Read has called "the forms of things unknown."[1] The concepts of analogy and metaphor come closer to the process of transferring knowledge from one domain to another, the "mental leaps" that underlie creativity. In contrast to the process of analysis, which begins with a very simple list of principles and definitions, almost a *tabula rasa*, to construct carefully, step by step, a rich world of new objects, the process of analogy creates unprecedented design through the rethinking of precedents. Most artists, architects, and even some engineers do not build their inventions on a *tabula rasa*. The new does not come from nowhere as much as the avant-garde has often claimed. In fact, unprecedented design often emerges from a thorough understanding of history. The best ally of invention is memory.

Looking at the work of Calatrava from this perspective, and considering the notebooks full of drawings of the hu-

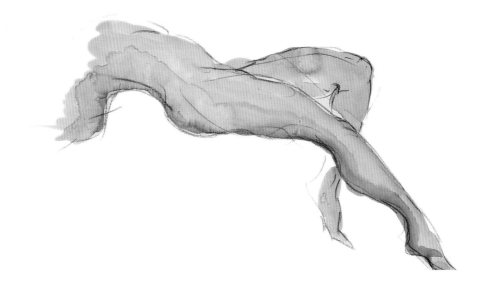

Above and facing page
Human figures

man body (33)—alone or in groups, loosely gestured or carefully detailed, and combined with bridges or buildings or animals—we see the role such precedents played as sources for analogies and metaphors in his architecture and engineering projects. Positions, gestures, profiles, skeletons and muscles, organs, skin, wings, and horns are constantly recalled, reinterpreted, and projected into project schemes. They invite new ways of looking at structure and enclosure. They make the unfamiliar familiar and make possible inventive solutions to difficult problems of program and site.

How can the body be envisioned as a building? How is an analogy drawn? For Calatrava the answer lies in another series of his artworks: the sculptures, which have been as important and as numerous as his figure sketches. Made of elementary parts—often cubes and prisms, rods, cables, or planar folded surfaces—they are the first level of the concrete through which Calatrava maps and matches forms and ideas, reframes bodies as design schemes, and begins to think metaphorically.

It is doubtful that the unfolding doors of the Ernsting Warehouse could have been designed without the analytical work of the ETH dissertation on transformation of space-frames. But it is equally debatable, if, in the same project, the reinterpretation of the "curtain wall" fluttering in the breeze, the lifting and bending "knee" joints, and the virtual movement of the wall, waving and pleating like cloth, could have come alive without the playful experiments in sculpture of 1993 and the memory of the architecture and sculpture of the temples of Greek antiquity.

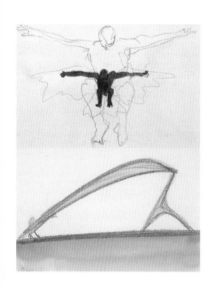

Above
Unfolding human figure (top)
Sculpture sketch (bottom)

Facing page
Sculpture in motion (top)
Pecking Bird sculpture (bottom)

The analytical investigation of the ETH dissertation and the analogical dream-work of the sketches and sculptures are two sides of the same coin, the "patient research," to quote Le Corbusier, needed for a designer to create. Art is the laboratory in which endless cycles of experimentation are carried out, resulting in both the realization of the most utilitarian projects and the creative metamorphosis of a pragmatic piece of infrastructure that is "dream-worked" into a living, aesthetic object. Analysis and analogy become two complements in Calatrava's poetics of movement. Design requires analysis to determine constraints and analogy to creatively produce within those constraints. Multiple analytical exercises and analogy experiments increase the rigor of the scientist and artist alike. Within Calatrava's chameleon scientist-artist identity, analysis and analogy become creative fulfillment.

Key in this interplay of analysis and analogy is the interaction between memory and invention. This principle of design thinking, so often ignored by designers, is exploited consistently by Calatrava in his poetics of movement. Building typology becomes operational as design awakens the mind. Like analysis and analogy, past experience (a prerequisite for invention) and invention (the essential condition for memory to be motivated) are complementary. Memory incites invention; invention invites memory.

Calatrava draws upon a range of art-historical precedents. His drawings of the human body in movement are reminiscent of Degas's and Rodin's drawings of dancers. Yet he differs from them in intention; his goal is to capture the

Above
Water sculpture in the landscape (top)
Wing sketch (middle)
Bird over water sketch (bottom)

Facing page
Sculpture (top)
Golden leaf sculpture (bottom)

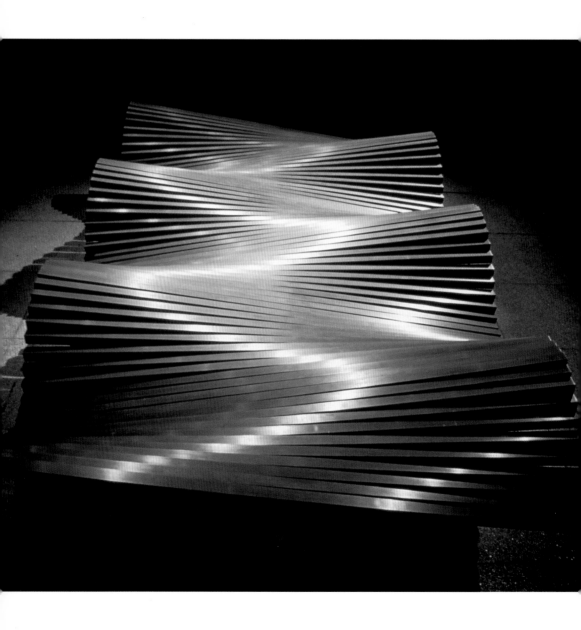

33: Drawings and Sculptures

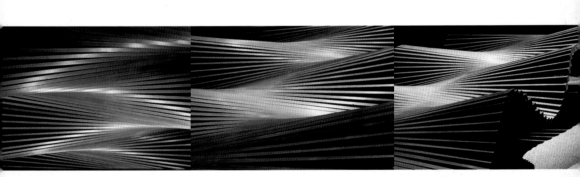

Above and facing page
Four views of Book in Flight sculpture

abstract morphology of moving figures. Similarly, although his sculptures bring to mind the work of Naum Gabo, Kenneth Snelson, Antoine Pevsner, Max Bill, David Smith, or Menashe Kadishman, Calatrava's abstract forms are unique in their intention to discover through abstract combinations of form the rules of morphology and movement of the concrete body in action. In combining both approaches, Calatrava's morphological investigations are close to the humanist, *homo universalis* tradition of Leonardo da Vinci and Goethe in their interest in understanding the structure of natural organisms and abstract forms and linking the structure to movement. In fact, Calatrava's use of mathematics brings him closer to da Vinci than to Goethe, who found mathematics inappropriate for analyzing organic nature.

We can envision movement in the form of any structure—even the most stable, such as an upright column—by projecting on it the diagram of operating forces and potential energy trapped within it, as D'Arcy Thompson invited us to do.[2] But movement in art was and is associated with breaking static compositional conventions and, further, with rejecting of institutionalized frameworks. In ancient Greek art the development of movement in figurative sculpture began with the gradual disengagement of the limbs from the pillarlike "block" of the human body, bringing one foot forward and bending the arms. Implied, of course, within this change is a redefinition of the archaic canons of structure. The famous fifth-century sculpture of an athlete, called in fact the Canon, by Polyclitus, and his book accompanying it, codified the representation of movement for centuries to come.[3] The book

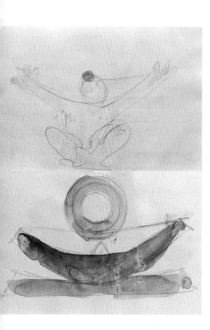

Above
Boy playing with a Slinky (top)
Sculpture study (bottom)

Facing page
Discerning Eye sculpture

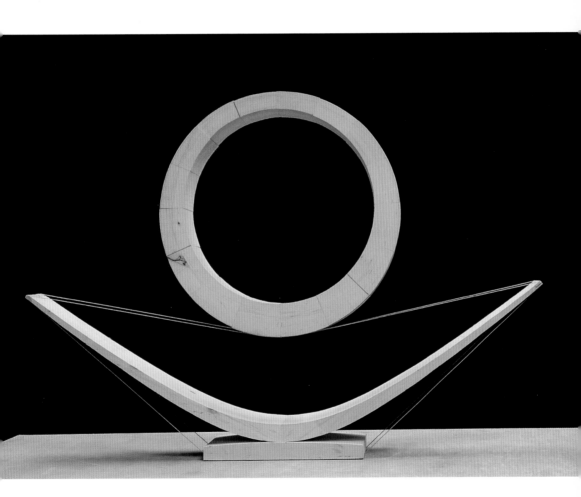

prescribed the ideal sculptural representation of the human body as resting on one leg, pushed a little to the rear, with the other a few inches in front and bent at the knee. The chest, while tilted backward, was slightly bent also, and the head leaned in the opposite direction of the chest. This "counterposing" of the limbs of the body was seen as a way of expressing graceful movement, a quality Polyclitus's sculptures were praised for.

More than a recipe for mimetic sculpture, the Canon created an abstract system of rules based on axes and a set of relationships between them to capture the most significant characteristics of any kind of human body in equilibrium while in motion. It was only in the Renaissance that a name, *contrapposto* ("counterposition"), was given to the Polyclitus configuration.[4] In choosing this term, the Renaissance design theoreticians, preoccupied with the idea of movement, combined two traditions—art and literature—to indicate that there was more in the relation between structure and movement than just change of position, and to express a more universal rule of poetics.[5]

Michelangelo, fascinated with creativity and the emergence of form rather than the static art product, is thought to have planned to write on movement. He was quoted praising the S-form "serpentine figure" as expressing "grace and loveliness" and as most appropriate to represent movement, which he called the *furia* of a figure. On closer inspection, the serpentine figure, the shape of the "flame of fire," was a very abstract, extreme geometric schematization of *contrapposto*. Gotthold Ephraim Lessing later devoted an entire book, on the famous Hellenistic

Above
Sketch study for table base in the form of interlocked bodies

Facing page
Sail or flame sculpture

Below
Preliminary sketch

Facing page
Overall view of tower

34

Montjuic Communications Tower

Barcelona, Spain, 1989–92

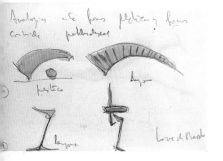

sculpture *Laocoön,* to the topic of the representation of movement in art and literature.[6] In it he introduced the concept of the "pregnant" moment.

Lessing's idea was that the artist, as opposed to the writer, "can use but a single moment of action … this single moment he makes as pregnant as possible" because within it he "unites two distinct points of time" by choosing the configuration most "suggestive of what has occurred before and what is to follow." This, of course, is the *contrapposto.*

Rarely has the concept of the pregnant moment been more clearly expressed in design than in Calatrava's leaning pylons and trusses, which appear to be either rising or falling, or in the "palindromic," flame-shaped columns, as Mannerists might have called them. Few designers of structures have explored the potential of *contrapposto* to relate movement to structure in the way that Calatrava has, in the complex profile of the pergola supports at the Stadelhofen Railway Station, leaning to reach out—a theme that recurs in different versions and scales in the Montjuic Communications Tower (34) and Alicante Tower (35), and in earlier works, including the railway station portico in Lucerne and the single arch of the La Devesa Footbridge in Ripoll.

Calatrava understands that even people with no architectural or engineering training have an intuitive understanding of the built physical environment. Through his use of our common-sense knowledge to read latent forces and potential movement in figures of sculpture or structure,

This page
Plan (left)
Side elevation (right)

Facing page
Detail of base (top)
Fountain (bottom)

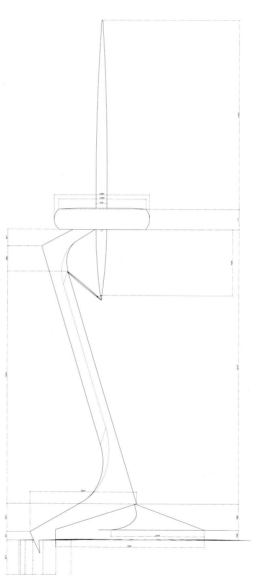

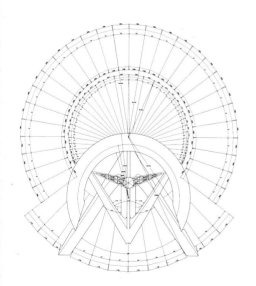

Facing page
Preliminary sketch

Calatrava invites the viewer to reflect, contemplate, and dream, and thus to become a part of the creative process as Michelangelo once envisaged.

To achieve this, the structure must go beyond problem-solving. It must go beyond optimization. While art is the laboratory for experimentation in making unfamiliar design problems familiar, it is also a means for *defamiliariz-ing* situations and, consequently, forcing us to rethink designs.[7] Like analysis and analogy, familiarization and defamiliarization become two complements in Calatrava's poetics of movement.

35

Alicante Tower

Alicante, Spain, 1993

Jean Piaget has observed that children in the most inten-sive stage of learning enjoy destroying structures more than assembling them. They throw objects, take them apart. This is how they understand the world not as a static, closed object, but as a universe of open and infinite possibilities. There is something playful in the structures of Calatrava, in his incorporation and manifestation of movement rather than the exclusion, suppression, or masking of it. Thus his work succeeds not only in the basic requirements of standing, containing, and covering with the minimum of resources, but also in achieving a cogni-tive provocation, the highest goal in the hierarchy of well-formed structures.

The structures, instead of only answering, reposit the question and restart the learning cycle. They reject didac-tic dogmas, perpetuating inquiry and inviting dream-work. But this dream-work transforms the narcissistic ten-dencies of aesthetic experience into a collective education

Preliminary sketches

about what exists, establishing a new paradigm for practice. They inspire wonder and keep dream-work alive. A
philosophical inquiry lies behind the obsession of form and
movement, memory and invention. Calatrava's poetics of
movement implicitly define a moral system for human
action and desire through his geometric reasoning. To
build community, a dialogue must begin between design
professionals and people who appreciate their built
environment, and wonder may be the ideal departure
point.

Notes

Introduction

1. A. Tzonis and L. Lefaivre, *Movement, Structure and the Work of Santiago Calatrava* (Basel, 1994).

2. B. Spinoza, *Ethics*, Part III (1678).

Chapter One

1. The key text is Galileo Galilei, *Two New Sciences* (Leiden, 1638). For further reading, see S. Shapin, *The Scientific Revolution* (1996), E. J. Dijksterjuis, *The Mechanization of the World Picture* (1961), and A. Tzonis and L. Lefaivre, "The Mechanical vs. Divine Body: The Rise of Modern Design Theory," *Journal of the Society of Architectural Historians* 3 (October 1975).

2. For the presence of rigorism in current architecture, see A. Tzonis and L. Lefaivre, *Architecture in North America since 1960* (Boston, 1995); and *Architecture in Europe since 1968: Memory and Invention* (New York, 1992).

3. Reported in A. Memmo, *Elementi d'Architettura Lodoliana* (Milan, 1833).

4. S. Calatrava Valls, *Zur Faltbarkheit von Fachwerken,* Ph.D. diss. (Zurich: ETH, 1981). Thesis advisors: Profs. Hans Brauchli and Herbert Krammel.

5. Ibid.

6. R. Courant and H. Robbins, *What Is Mathematics?* (New York, 1941), p. 155.

Chapter Two

1. Optimization here is meant in a more qualitative sense, indicating a design stance rather than a strict mathematical calculation.

2. Galileo Galilei, *Two New Sciences* (Leiden, 1638).

3. G. Semper, "Style: The Textile Art," in *The Four Elements of Architecture and Other Writings*, trans. H.F. Mallgrave and W. Herrmann (Cambridge, 1989), pp. 254ff.

4. A. Tzonis and L. Lefaivre, *Movement, Structure and the Work of Santiago Calatrava* (Basel, 1994).

5. See L. Mumford, "Surrealism and Civilization," *New Yorker* (December 19, 1936), about the Surrealist exhibition at the Museum of Modern Art in New York.

Chapter Four

1. The idea of the leaning single pylon is already formed for the Caballros Bridge in Lérida, Spain, designed in 1985 but never built. The concept emerged out of the constraints imposed by the site permitting only a single pier on stable ground.

Chapter Six

1. H. Read, *The Forms of Things Unknown* (Ohio, 1963).

2. D.W. Thompson, *On Growth and Form* (1942; rev. ed., New York, 1992).

3. A. Tzonis and L. Lefaivre, *Movement, Structure and the Work of Santiago Calatrava* (Basel, 1994).

4. Quintilian, *Institutio Oratoria*, trans. H.E. Butler (1920; reprint, Cambridge, Mass., 1980).

5. G.P. Lomazzo, *Trattato dell'arte della pittura* (1584).

6. G.E. Lessing, *Laocoon: An Essay upon the Limits of Painting and Poetry* (orig. publ. in German, 1766; New York, 1957).

7. A. Tzonis and L. Lefaivre, *Classical Architecture*.

Selected Bibliography

Books

Blaser, W., *Santiago Calatrava: Ingenieur Architektur, Engineering Architecture* (Basel: Birkhauser Verlag, 1989).

Frampton, K., et al., *Calatrava Bridges* (Zurich: Artemis Verlag, 1993).

Harbison, R., *Creatures from the Mind of the Engineer: The Architecture of Santiago Calatrava* (Zurich: Artemis Verlag, 1992).

Klein, B., *Santiago Calatrava: Bahnhof Stadelhofen, Zurich* (Berlin: Wasmuth Verlag, 1993).

Sharp, D., *Santiago Calatrava* (London: Book Art/E&FN Spon, 1992).

Tischauser, A., and S. von Moss, *Public Buildings* (Basel: Birkhauser Verlag, 1998).

Tzonis, A., and L. Lefaivre, *Movement, Structure and the Work of Santiago Calatrava* (Basel: Birkhauser Verlag 1994).

Webster, A.C., and K. Frampton, *Santiago Calatrava: Schule und Museum fur Gestaltung* (Zurich: Schriftenreihe 15, 1992).

Zardini, M., and F. Motta, *Santiago Calatrava* (Milan: Libro Segreto, 1995).

Catalogues, Special Issues, Project Monographs

Calatrava, Santiago, *Dynamische Gleichgewichte: neue Projekte* (Zurich: Artemis Verlag, 1991).

Cullen, M.S., and M. Kieren, *Calatrava: Berlin Five Projects* (Basel: Birkhauser Verlag, 1994).

Hauser, Hobe, *Kontroverse Beitrage zu einem unstrittenen Bautypus* (Stuttgart: 1993).

Le Roux, M., and M. Rivoire, *Calatrava* (Grenoble: Escale Satolas, 1994).

McQuaid, M., *Santiago Calatrava: Structure and Expression* (New York: Museum of Modern Art, 1993).

Molinari, L., *Santiago Calatrava* (Milan: Skira, 1998).

Nicolin, P., "Santiago Calatrava, Il folle volo" (*Quaderni di Lotus 7*, Milan: Electa, 1987).

Polano, S., *Santiago Calatrava*, Documenti di Architettura (Milan: Electa, 1996).

Santiago Calatrava (Valencia, Spain: Generalitat Valenciana, 1986).

Santiago Calatrava (Zurich: Galerie Jamilch Weber, 1986).

"Santiago Calatrava 1983–93" (Valencia: 1993; reprinted as an editorial in *El Croquis*, Madrid, 1993).

Santiago Calatrava: El Croquis, vol. 47 (Madrid: 1992).

Santiago Calatrava: El Croquis, vol. 38 (Madrid: 1989).

Santiago Calatrava, 1983–1996 (Madrid: AV-Monografias, 1996).

Santiago Calatrava: The Dynamics of Equilibrium (Tokyo: Ma Gallery, 1994).

List of Projects